Master the Game
Midfielder

Master the Game
Midfielder

Paul Broadbent and Andrew Allen

HODDER
EDUCATION
PART OF HACHETTE LIVRE UK

All photographs have been provided by Action Images Ltd.

Fitness Disclaimer
The information in this book is designed only to help you make informed decisions about health and fitness. It is not intended as any kind of substitute for the advice or treatment that may have been prescribed by your doctor.

Before following any of the information or recommendations in this book, you should get an assessment of your overall health from your doctor to ensure that it's safe for you to exercise.

You're solely responsible for the way you view and use the information in this book, and do so at your own risk. The authors are not responsible in any way for any kind of injuries or health problems that might occur due to using this book or following the advice in it.

Every effort has been made to trace the correct copyright holders of this work, but if any have been inadvertently overlooked the publisher will be pleased to make the necessary arrangements at the first opportunity.

Orders: please contact Bookpoint Ltd, 130 Milton Park, Abingdon, Oxon OX14 4SB. Telephone: (44) 01235 827720. Fax: (44) 01235 400454. Lines are open from 9.00–5.00, Monday to Saturday, with a 24-hour message answering service. You can also order through our website www.hoddereducation.co.uk.

British Library Cataloguing in Publication Data
A catalogue record for this title is available from the British Library.

ISBN-13: 978 034092 8417

First Published   2008
Impression number   10 9 8 7 6 5 4 3 2 1
Year   2012 2011 2010 2009 2008

Hachette Livre UK's policy is to use papers that are natural, renewable and recyclable products and made from wood grown in sustainable forests. The logging and manufacturing processes are expected to conform to the environmental regulations of the country of origin.

Typeset by Servis Filmsetting Ltd, Manchester.
Printed in Great Britain for Hodder Education, part of Hachette Livre UK,
338 Euston Road, London NW1 3BH by Cox and Wyman Ltd, Reading, Berkshire.

Contents

Introduction

Football is without doubt the most popular sport in the world. In a recent survey carried out by FIFA (Fédération Internationale de Football Association), the world football governing body, it was estimated that there are 265 million male and female players worldwide. A pleasing sign in this survey is the continuing growth of the women's game. Over recent years, girls' football in particular has seen a massive growth in popularity and has now become the fastest growing sport for girls.

For many young people, football is played in order to 'live the dream' of becoming a professional player. This only becomes a reality for a small percentage, so in most cases the appeal of the game is largely social and for pure enjoyment, with the added health benefit of increased fitness. Whatever the reason, all young footballers aspire to play at their highest level and full potential. It is not uncommon for a keen young footballer to go through their early playing career without the regular support of a qualified football coach. These players, however, are still keen to improve their skills and develop their game.

This book has been written to support players to reach their full potential, allowing all young footballers to develop their game either on their own or with their friends. Following the practices and drills within the book, reading the top tips and testing themselves at the end of each chapter will give young players the opportunity to increase their knowledge and develop their game.

It is widely accepted that the more you practise, the better your game will become. This applies to football just as much as it does to any other sport. Knowing the correct techniques, understanding and applying tactical elements and analysing team play will allow young players to develop their game and improve their chances of success.

This book is one of a series of four books covering four key positions within the modern game: Goalkeeper, Defender, Midfielder and Striker. Each book contains tips, drills, practices and techniques applicable to the respective positions. There are also chapters within each book that will be of general interest to all footballers that relate to fitness, diet, equipment and dealing with injuries, as well as advice on finding the right club.

Football can certainly be 'a beautiful game' as Pele once famously stated. With careful physical and mental preparation, increased understanding of the game and relevant practice of skills and techniques, you can play your part in this wonderful sport. We hope you enjoy the book and that it helps you achieve your potential as a footballer.

Paul Broadbent and Andrew Allen

Part 1

Introducing the game

Chapter 1

Playing the game

THIS CHAPTER WILL:
- Explain the principles of play.
- Describe team formations and systems.
- Give an understanding of what it takes to become a midfielder.

Principles of play

Playing football is all about attacking and defending, individually and as a team. The principles of playing football depend on whether your team are in possession of the ball, or the other team has possession. If your team is in possession of the football you will be concerned with the **attacking principles of play**. All the players in your team will support the attack, as a unit, with specific responsibilities for each player depending on their individual position and where the ball is at the time.

If your team is not in possession of the football, you will be concerned with the **defending principles of play**. All the players in your team will have defensive responsibilities, as a unit, with specific

All players should support the attack.

responsibilities for each player, once again, depending on their individual position and where the ball is.

Attacking principles

Attacking principles of play are about players creating space and then making the most of this space as an individual and as a team. For this to happen, your team needs to be in possession of the football. For it to happen effectively, you will need to consider the following points:

- **Creating space by spreading out – side to side.** It is important to try to create space both in between and behind defenders and this should happen as soon as possible after your team gains possession. If it is done quickly, it gives the opposition little time to man mark and cover each other. Players should try to see everything that is happening on the pitch as they spread out, and should not turn their back on the ball. Having stretched out side to side, your team should look to progress forward as quickly as possible.

All players have defensive responsibilities.

- **Creating space by spreading out – end to end.** Teams should also look to get their players to spread out end to end as well as side to side. This requires the player furthest away from the ball to make a run towards it, creating space behind them to be used by other players running off the ball into the space. Overlapping runs create space, and can take place on the wings and in central positions.

- **One-touch play.** One-touch play is an extremely effective attacking tactic as it does not allow the opposition time to pressurize you and your team-mates. One-touch play requires players to have an excellent understanding of support and movement on and off the ball. Quick one-touch play, coupled with good movement, can make it very difficult for defenders to mark players and keep a tight formation. The 'wall-pass' (or 'give and go') is a common one-touch play in football. Passing the ball to a team-mate who plays it back to you, one touch, as you go forward and exploit the space in front of you, is an effective pass for attacking play.

Wall-pass

Another example of a one-touch pass and move play that can be very effective is called 'third man running'. This involves three players – a passer, a receiver and a runner. The ball is played up to the receiver, laid off at an angle to the passer and played one touch into the path of the runner.

- **Changing direction of play.** Players with the ability to see and then deliver a long diagonal pass from wing to wing can create and set up an opportunity to exploit space and change the direction of play. Another effective way of changing the direction of play occurs when players make cross-over runs, pulling defenders out of position and creating space behind them. Another example is reverse passing, with players changing the direction of play by running with the ball in one direction and passing it in the opposite direction.

- **Dribbling.** Dribbling is a very exciting attacking principle and is often used in the last third of the pitch. A player who can take on, and beat other players, or draw in defenders, creates space if the ball is delivered at the right time for team-mates to exploit. If a player can take on and go past a defender it also creates a numerical advantage for their team.

Defending principles

Defending principles of play are about denying space to the team in possession. The defending team attempts to get all its players back behind the ball, applying pressure to the player in possession both individually and as a team.

- **Denying the opposition space.** Two principles at the heart of good defensive play are **compactness** and **quantity**. In order to prevent the opposition from scoring, the defence has to be compactly organized, blocking the opposition's direct path to goal. Getting players back behind the ball and being compact as a unit makes it harder for the attackers to develop goal-scoring opportunities and generally forces them out to the wings. It is also important for the defending team to get as many players back behind the ball as possible, to outnumber the offensive players. This is why strikers and midfield players need to drop behind the ball when their team loses possession and for full-backs and other defenders to try to delay the attack by 'jockeying' so these players have time to run back – jockeying is keeping your body between the attacker and the goal, backing off slightly as the attacker moves forward and waiting for the right moment to tackle.

- **Applying pressure.** Pressurizing the ball is the first principle of defensive play, making it harder for the team in possession to develop their attacking play. Pressurizing the ball is most important to reduce the scoring opportunities when play is close to your own team's goal. Successfully applying pressure, particularly as a team, often leads to a regain of possession. The level of pressure is a decision that needs to be made by a defender in each situation. It may be that the defender needs to 'jockey' the player, delaying and slowing the player down until there are enough defenders to support and cover them. If the player is running with the ball in front of them, it may be appropriate to carry out a well-timed tackle. Applying pressure in whatever form is a team responsibility. Without your team being able to shut or close down the outlet pass, there can be little point in individuals pressurizing the ball. An element of applying pressure involves 'marking' the attacking team players.

This could mean staying very close to a specific player, or holding a formation so that if the ball comes into your area you get to the ball before an attacking player. Correct and thoughtful marking of players puts pressure on attacking players and denies them space to play.

• **Pressure, cover and balance.** Pressure, cover and balance refers to the responsibilities of the first, second and third defenders. The **first defender** is the defender that is close enough to the ball to put pressure on the ball, to possibly tackle or to delay the attacker, denying them the opportunity to play the ball forward to their team-mates. This first defender may be a striker in your team. It will all depend on where the ball is at the time. The **second defender** is any defender who is close enough to cover space behind the first defender, who can step in and defend against the attacker if the first defender is beaten. All other players are **third defenders**. These are defenders who are not close enough to pressure the ball or to cover the space behind the first defender. Third defenders provide 'balance' so that, while other defenders apply pressure to try to win the ball, third defenders cover space on areas of the pitch away from the ball. Third defenders also track runners who run at a space behind the defence.

Transition phase

Moving from defence into attack or attack into defence when possession changes is called the 'transition phase'. This can be a crucial part of the game. If a team is slow to get back to defend and set their defensive positions after they have lost the ball, the opposing team can quickly attack on the break, taking advantage of the space left on the pitch. Alternatively, a team that wins the ball and turns defence into attack needs its players to be quick-thinking, making decisive runs into attacking spaces. It is important that all players, in all positions, know their responsibilities as attackers and defenders. Concentration is important, so when there is a change of possession each player knows what his or her or role is within the team, so that they act quickly and effectively.

Your role in a team

Whether your team is attacking (in possession) or defending (not in possession), you are likely to have certain responsibilities that will help your team. These responsibilities will vary depending on the position you play in your team and also depending on where the ball is lost and regained.

Tables 1.1 and 1.2 show some of the responsibilities that you will have as a midfielder, depending on whether you are attacking or defending.

Team formations and systems

Team formations and systems are, in simple terms, how a team lines up at kick off and how they attempt to keep this team shape throughout the game. Coaches often ask what the 'best formation' is. There isn't one. A formation is supposed to make best use of the players' abilities within a team. What works best for a team depends on what their strengths are and what kind of players are available. It may also depend on factors such as playing against a strong attacking team or even weather conditions.

Table 1.1 **Wide midfielders**

Attacking	Defending
Try to link with forwards on your side of the pitch	Get behind the ball as soon as possible
Make penetrating runs into the space left by forwards' movements	Track back any opposing midfielder runs
Hold your position and try to attack from wide positions	Try to keep the ball in one part of the pitch by closing down and forcing the direction of play
Move infield, but keep team shape when the ball is on the opposite side of the pitch	Be prepared to cover for central midfielders if they have gone forward to join an attack

Table 1.2 **Central midfielders**

Attacking	Defending
Try to support and link up with the players around you – forwards, wide midfielders and full-backs	Get behind the ball as soon as possible and apply pressure
You will often dictate attacking play by the quality and choice of pass	Track back, and be aware of opposing midfielders penetrating runs
Try to get forward to join the attack by linking up with the forwards and making runs into the space behind them	Be prepared to cover for full-backs and central defenders if they join an attack
	Look to start the attack by picking up clearances by the opposition

Top tips

- A good formation will help a good team, but skill and awareness count for much more.
- Whatever formation your team plays, it is vital that you stay in touch with all team-mates with good communication.
- Be prepared for your formation to change during a game – this decision will be made by your coach rather than the players.

Key to formations

GK	Goalkeeper
RB	Right-back
LB	Left-back
CD	Central defender
RM	Right midfielder
LM	Left midfielder
CM	Central midfielder
CF	Centre-forward
LF	Left-forward
RF	Right-forward

The 4-4-2 formation

The 4-4-2 formation is probably the most common one in the modern game, with a good balance throughout the positions. Four defenders and four midfielders will often mean eight players behind the ball when defending. The four midfielders are also available to support the two forwards when attacking. It can be an effective attacking formation, especially if you have two strong forwards who can outrun the opposition defence and fast attacking midfielders to support them. However, with only two attackers playing up front, this alone is not enough to stretch apart a defensive line of usually four opponents. The two wide midfielders provide automatic width to the midfield and attacking shape of the team. The use of four defenders adds compactness and balance in the back, where either the sweeper or the flat back four can be utilized.

Figure 1.1 **The 4-4-2 formation**

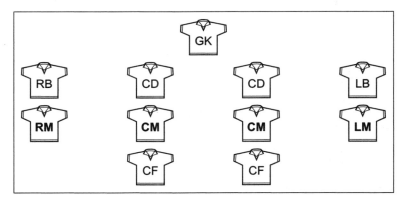

The role of the four midfielders as a unit

The four midfield players are the link between defenders and strikers and must perform from penalty area to penalty area. As well as attacking as a winger, the wide midfielder will often have to cover back and around and act as a fifth defender when opponents are attacking on the opposite side of the pitch. Generally, the two central midfield players look to hold their position in the centre of the field.

As one of the two central midfielders you should:

- **Be part of one unit across the middle of the pitch with the two wide midfielders, and also up and down the pitch with defenders and forwards.**

- **Try to keep the team shape, linking play and not becoming isolated.**

- Dictate the pace of the game by increasing and lowering the tempo depending on the match circumstances.
- Look to get forward, making penetrating runs into the attacking third of the pitch.
- Provide a range of quality passes to team-mates – short passes to striker's feet and also longer passes into the areas behind the opponents' defenders.
- Use 'give and go' passes around the pitch to link up with both midfielders and strikers.
- Look for the best forward option by playing with head up in order to see and assess passing options.
- Be prepared to provide defensive cover for wide midfielders and full-backs who may have gone forward.
- Track back, particularly watching for penetrating runs from opponents' midfield players.

As one of the two wide midfielders you should:

- Be part of one midfield unit across the middle of the pitch with central midfielders but also play as one unit up and down the pitch with wide defender and wide forward.
- Be prepared to provide defensive cover when opponents are attacking on the opposite side of the pitch.
- Look to support attacks by getting into forward positions, and if your team is attacking on the opposite side, try and make blind-sided runs behind the nearest defender.
- Have the technical ability to provide a range of different crosses to the near and far post and, when appropriate, look to deliver early crosses to forwards.

The 3-5-2 formation

The 3-5-2 formation is more attacking than the 4-4-2 formation, as it moves forward the 'fourth full-back' who often may have minimal defending to do against only two attackers. With only three at the back, defenders must be solid and work together as a unit. Often a midfield player may be called upon to support the defence. A coach may often consider a 3-5-2 formation if they have an abundance of midfield players. Like all systems it needs to be able to operate when defending and attacking. Using this formation, teams will often defend and attack in two units – the back three and midfield five when defending and the midfield five and two forwards when attacking.

Figure 1.2 **The 3-5-2 formation**

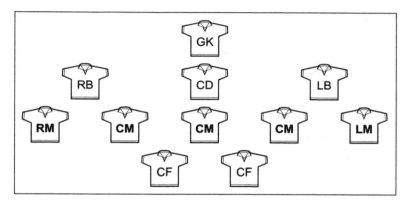

The role of the five midfielders as a unit

The five midfield players are the link between defenders and strikers and must perform from penalty area to penalty area. The wide midfielder will often have to cover back and around and act as a fourth defender when opponents are attacking on the opposite side of the pitch.

Generally, the three central midfield players look to hold their position in the centre of the field and one central midfielder must hold a deep position to stop any counter-attack when possession is lost, particularly if the wide midfielders have both moved into advanced positions.

As one of the three central midfielders you should:

- Be part of one unit across the middle of the pitch with the two wide midfielders and also up and down the pitch with defenders and forwards.
- Try to keep the team shape, linking play and not becoming isolated.
- Dictate the pace of the game by increasing and lowering the tempo depending on the match circumstances.
- Look to get forward, making penetrating runs into the attacking third of the pitch.
- Get possession of the ball from defenders and move it forward.
- Provide a range of quality passes to team-mates – short passes to striker's feet and also longer passes into the areas behind the opponents' defenders.
- Use 'give and go' passes around the pitch, to link up with both midfielders and strikers.
- Look for the best forward option by playing with head up in order to see and assess passing options.
- Be prepared to provide defensive cover for wide midfielders and full-backs who may have gone forward.
- Track back, particularly watching for penetrating runs from opponents' midfield players.

As one of the two wide midfielders you should:

- Be part of one midfield unit across the middle of the pitch with the three central midfielders but also play as one unit up and down the pitch with wide defender and wide forward.
- Be prepared to provide defensive cover when opponents are attacking on the opposite side of the pitch.
- Create width in attack.
- Look to support attacks by getting into forward positions. If your team is attacking on the opposite side, try to make blind-sided runs behind the nearest defender.
- Provide a range of different crosses to the near and far post and, when appropriate, look to deliver early crosses to forwards.

The 4-5-1 formation

The 4-5-1 and 4-3-3 formations are very similar, with the 4-5-1 being a defensive set-up that can easily switch into a 4-3-3 if necessary. The nature of the positioning of the players makes it a very difficult system to break down, particularly if the team remains well organized and disciplined. With the midfield packed and compact, it is good for keeping possession of the ball through a series of short passes, occasionally linking up with the lone forward. In attacking terms, there is a real emphasis on the midfield players to get forward to support the lone striker. The wingbacks (wide midfield players) provide instant width in attack and good defensive cover in these wide positions. The wingbacks can also be used to bring the ball out of defence. The system may see the back four defenders playing with a sweeper or a 'flat back four'.

Figure 1.3 **The 4-5-1 formation**

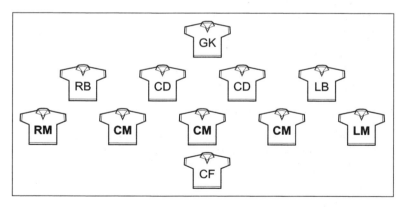

The role of the five midfielders as a unit

The five midfield players are the link between defenders and strikers and must perform from penalty area to penalty area. The wide midfielder will often have to cover back and around and act as a fifth defender when opponents are attacking on the opposite side of the pitch.

Generally, the three central midfield players look to hold their position in the centre of the field and one central midfielder must hold a deep position to stop any counter-attack when possession is lost, particularly if the wide midfielders have both got into advanced positions.

As one of the three central midfielders you should:

- Be part of one unit across the middle of the pitch with the two wide midfielders and also up and down the pitch with defenders and forwards.

- Try to keep the team shape, linking play and not becoming isolated.

- Dictate the pace of the game by increasing and lowering the tempo depending on the match circumstances.

- Look to get forward, making penetrating runs into the attacking third of the pitch.

- Get possession of the ball from defenders and move it forward.

- Provide a range of quality passes to team-mates – short passes to striker's feet and also longer passes into the areas behind the opponents' defenders.

- Use 'give and go' passes around the pitch, to link up with both midfielders and strikers.

- Look for the best forward option by playing with head up in order to see and assess passing options.

- Be prepared to provide defensive cover for wide midfielders and full-backs who may have gone forward.

- Be prepared to play in a deep defensive position to stop swift counter-attacking.

- Track back, particularly watching for penetrating runs from opponents' midfield players.

As one of the two wide midfielders you should:

- Be part of one midfield unit across the middle of the pitch with the three central midfielders but also play as one unit up and down the pitch with wide defender and wide forward.

- Be prepared to provide defensive cover when opponents are attacking on the opposite side of the pitch.

- Create width in attack.

- Look to support attacks by getting into forward positions, and if your team is attacking on the opposite side, try to make blind-sided runs behind the nearest defender.

- Provide a range of different crosses to the near and far post and, when appropriate, look to deliver early crosses to forwards.

The 4-3-3 formation

Teams playing a 4-3-3 formation are likely to be playing a narrow game through the middle of the pitch, although when the ball is on their side of the pitch, the full-back and wide midfield player should be encouraged to take up wide positions to provide width in the attack. The two full-backs are able to provide automatic width when building play from the back. With 4-3-3, teams need to encourage the wide forwards to drop back to help with the build-up. One of the benefits of this formation for younger players is that they often look to force the ball through the middle of the field, whereas this system encourages them to build attacks by playing the ball forward into the wide channels rather than simply through the middle.

Figure 1.4 **The 4-3-3 formation**

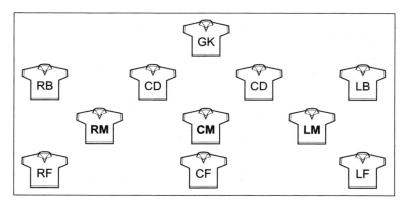

The role of the three midfielders as a unit

The three midfield players are the link between the defenders and the strikers. Hard working, they must perform from penalty area to penalty area. With only three midfield players it is essential that they keep their shape and generally look to support the strikers from behind rather than by making runs beyond them.

As one of the three midfielders you should:

- Be part of one unit across the middle of the pitch, interchanging positions with each other and also up and down the pitch, linking with defenders and strikers.
- Try to keep the team shape, linking play and not becoming isolated.
- Dictate the pace of the game by increasing and lowering the tempo depending on the match circumstances.
- Look to get forward, making penetrating runs into the attacking third of the pitch.
- Get possession of the ball from defenders and move it forward.
- Provide a range of quality passes to team-mates – short passes to striker's feet and also longer passes into the areas behind the opponents' defenders.
- Use 'give and go' passes around the pitch to link up with both midfielders and strikers.
- Look for the best forward option by playing with head up in order to see and assess passing options.
- Be prepared to provide defensive cover for wide midfielders and full-backs who may have gone forward.
- Be prepared to remain in a deep defensive position to stop swift counter-attacking play.
- Track back, particularly watching for penetrating runs from opponents' midfield players.

The 3-4-3 formation

The 3-4-3 formation is considered to be an attacking formation when in possession of the ball, and also lends itself to a high pressure style of defending without the ball. Using this formation, teams can easily attack and defend with a minimum number of seven players: either the back three and four midfield players when defending or the midfield four and the three forwards when attacking. Normally the central striker will consistently stay at the tip of the attack while one midfield player will often protect the back three by constantly pressurizing the ball to help the defence.

Figure 1.5 **The 3-4-3 formation**

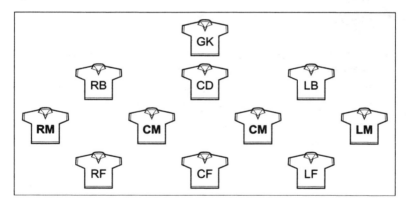

The role of the four midfielders as a unit

The four midfield players are the link between defenders and strikers and must perform from penalty area to penalty area. The wide midfielder will often have to cover back and around and act as a fourth defender when opponents are attacking on the opposite side of the pitch. Generally, the two central midfield players look to hold their position in the centre of the field.

As one of the two central midfielders you should:

- Be part of one unit across the middle of the pitch with the two wide midfielders and also up and down the pitch with defenders and forwards.

- Try to keep the team shape, linking play and not becoming isolated.

- Dictate the pace of the game by increasing and lowering the tempo depending on the match circumstances.

- Look to get forward, making penetrating runs into the attacking third of the pitch.

- Provide a range of quality passes to team-mates – short passes to striker's feet and also longer passes into the areas behind the opponents' defenders.

- Use 'give and go' passes around the pitch to link up with both midfielders and strikers.

- Look for the best forward option by playing with head up in order to see and assess passing options.

- Be prepared to provide defensive cover for wide midfielders and full-backs who may have gone forward.

- Track back, particularly watching for penetrating runs from opponents' midfield players.

As one of the two wide midfielders you should:

- Be part of one midfield unit across the middle of the pitch with central midfielders, but also play as one unit up and down the pitch with wide defender and wide forward.

- Be prepared to provide defensive cover when opponents are attacking on the opposite side of the pitch.

- Look to support attacks by getting into forward positions. If your team is attacking on the opposite side, try and make blind-sided runs behind the nearest defender.

- Provide a range of different crosses to the near and far post and, when appropriate, look to deliver early crosses to forwards.

The advantages and disadvantages of various formations

Table 1.3 **Advantages and disadvantages of various formations**

	4-4-2	3-5-2	4-5-1	4-3-3	3-4-3
Defensive strength	Four players when defending provides cover of all space.	Usually one central midfielder sits in front of the back three. This gives good cover of central space.	Very strong defensive unit, but does depend on how many players are pushed forward to attack.	Covers the space well. Also good for stopping opposition playing out from back.	Good coverage of the central areas of defence, though without central support from midfield to sit in front of the back three.
Defensive weakness	Fewer players in the central areas.	Three defenders instead of four means 25 per cent extra space for two wide forwards to exploit.	Only one forward means the opposition have real opportunity to play the ball in their defensive third.	Fewer players in the central areas and less support for full-backs on the transition phase.	Even though strong centrally, extra space for two wide forwards to exploit.

Table 1.3 **(continued)**

	4-4-2	3-5-2	4-5-1	4-3-3	3-4-3
Playing out from the back	The two full-backs start in excellent positions to offer this option to their team.	With only three at the back, it means that wingbacks need to drop back, though this then gives them fewer passing options.	This formation provides several options, though the position will often push a full-back forward into midfield to try and counter this.	The two full-backs start in excellent positions to offer this option to their team, though less wide support for the next pass. Often sees teams playing a longer pass forward.	With only three at the back it does not offer the options for players to receive the ball in wide positions.
Effect on midfield	Provides a diamond or flat shape to the midfield when attacking or defending. If outnumbered in midfield, sometimes a full-back will be pushed into midfield.	The central midfield area will often have a numerical advantage – three to two.	This formation provides several options to the midfield – often three midfield players will support the forward (two wide and one central).	The three midfield players are likely to be central, which means the team may require two of the forwards to drop back to help in the wider areas of the pitch.	Provides a diamond or flat shape to the midfield. If outnumbered in midfield, it will require one of the forward players to drop back to support the midfield.

Effect on forwards	The midfield and full-backs need to be willing to get forward to support the forwards.	Provides good central support for runs beyond the forwards.	Really needs a forward who is good at holding the ball up and bringing the midfielders in to the game.	Numerically, it suggests that three forwards offer you more, though depends on how much dropping back the two wide forwards have to do.	Numerically it suggests that three forwards offer you more, though depends on the amount of defensive duty required from the wide forwards.
Overall	Strong defensively and can be good for playing out from the back. Best formation for using the full width of the pitch.	Strong centrally and in central midfield – vulnerable to width at the back.	A relatively defensive formation. The team needs to be able to build play well and have a forward who can hold the ball up well.	Good for stopping opposition's full-backs from playing. Offers less width for playing out from the back, but can offer width in attack.	Strong centrally, in defensive areas, and good formation for using width in midfield. Three forwards provide width in attack.

What it takes to become a midfielder

Whatever your favoured position, or the position that you are asked to play by your coach, you will need a range of technical, physical and psychological skills and attributes. Many of these are relevant to more than one position. For example, a good midfielder will need to have the ability to get forward and join an attack, and also to be able to defend and tackle for their team. Therefore, they will need to develop their skills and attributes to suit the demands of defending and attacking play.

Quote

'In a good midfield player, you will see someone with an attitude to want to go past and beyond players, willing to tackle back, willing to help their team-mates, a mental strength to cope with crowd pressure, an ability to dribble, score goals, play off either foot, someone who is brave, has a tactical awareness and the ability to influence others. Two great examples in the modern game are Frank Lampard and Steven Gerrard.'
  (Adrian Boothroyd)

From research and player observation, it has been identified that 'good midfielders' are likely to have the attributes listed in Table 1.4 for wide, creative and holding midfielders. Almost all of these attributes can be developed and improved with practice and support from your coach.

Table 1.4 **Attributes of good midfielders**

	Wide midfielder	Creative midfielder	Holding midfielder
Technique (when team in possession)	• Good attacking skills in 1 v 1 situation • Flair for attack • Dribbling skills • Good crossing ability	• Excellent receiving skills • Good distribution • High all-round skill • Dribbling skills • Inventive turns • Good touch	• Good passing and distribution • Combination play • Dribbling skills • Receive the ball with both feet • Support full-backs and wide midfielders
Technique (when team not in possession)	• Discipline in defence • Tackling skills • Support and cover	• Tackling skills • Good at 1 v 1 • Support and cover	• Strong in the tackle • Good defending 1 v 1 • Support and cover • Excellent pressurizing
Physical	• Good fitness levels • Forward runs • Quick, athletic • Willingness to track back	• High fitness levels • Quick • Strong	• Stamina • Willingness to track back • Quick • Strong
Mental psychological	• Never gives in	• Confidence • Awareness • Intelligence • Imagination	• Competitive • Never gives in • Communicates • Aggressive

Summary

- Whatever position you play you need to understand the attacking and defending principles of play.

- Players need to try to create space when they are attacking and deny space to the opposition when they are defending.

- You need to be clear about your roles and responsibilities in the team whether attacking or defending.

- A team formation, such as 4-4-2, shows the shape that a team keeps throughout the game. Any formation needs to be flexible and to make best use of the players' abilities.

Self testers

1 Describe the tactic of 'third man running'.
2 What is the role of the 'second defender'?
3 What are the advantages of playing a 4–3–3 formation?
4 Give three attributes of a good 'holding midfielder'.

Action plan

1 Using Table 1.4, consider how you match up to the skills and attributes for the position you play.
2 Use this book to find out how you can improve your technique and understanding for the position you play.
3 With the support of your teacher or coach, evaluate your performance and develop a goal-setting programme.

Part 2

Preparing for the game

Chapter 2

Fitness for football

THIS CHAPTER WILL:
- Give an understanding of the key elements that make up general fitness.
- Consider the specific elements of fitness that you need as a footballer.
- Outline the importance of exercise to keep fit.

Match fit

You may know from experience that football can be a physically demanding sport. If you monitored the types of movements that you made during a match it would make an impressive list:

- sprinting
- jogging
- walking
- running backwards
- running sideways
- accelerating
- jumping
- kicking
- turning
- stretching.

All these movements are very difficult if you haven't got a basic level of general fitness as well as a specific fitness suited to football.

Statistic

A professional footballer runs between 8 and 13 km in a match.

The four Ss

Players with good skills, technique and motivation may be 'natural' footballers, but if they are short of general fitness then the player is unlikely to reach his or her potential. To be generally fit and healthy and able to do everyday physical activities without feeling tired, you need the four Ss:

Figure 2.1 **The four Ss**

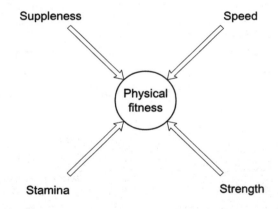

Speed – a big part of the game, not just for short sprints but also for longer concentrated spells.

Strength – many skills in football can be helped with physical strength, both for the upper and lower body.

Stamina – football is a high-intensity sport played over a long period and players need to last the full 90 minutes in a match.

Suppleness – flexibility is important because of the wide range of movements required when playing football.

Specific fitness

As well as a good level of general fitness, you need to have specific fitness to play football at a high level. These are the elements of fitness that can make the difference between a good player and a world-class player:

- **Agility** – in a match you may turn and change direction 400–500 times, so you need to be able to move and turn quickly and easily.

- **Quick reactions** – you need to respond quickly to constant and sudden changes in play.

- **Balance** – with the ball at your feet and a defender putting you under pressure, you need to be balanced and steady in order to keep possession, pass or shoot.

- **Coordination** – there are a number of different techniques and movements involved in passing, shooting or tackling. These rely on different parts of the body working together smoothly and efficiently.

- **Timing** – you need to act at just the right moment, with good timing for your runs, tackles or passes.

There are also specific elements of fitness that players in different positions in a team will need. A goalkeeper will have different requirements to a striker, and even within the midfield position there are different roles. See p. 27 to find out about the key attributes of a wide creative and holding midfielder.

Holding midfielder

In this position you will be required to constantly put pressure on the opponent's midfielders and therefore cover a lot of ground. You will also be looking to support your defence when in possession and you may have little time for rest and recovery. This means that excellent stamina is vital if you play as a holding midfielder. You will also need to be physically strong and quick to hold up the opposition players and make decisive tackles.

Creative midfielder

Speed and stamina are both critical elements of fitness if you play this role in a team. You need to be a quick player – able to combine your defensive midfield role with bursts forward to support your strikers. It may be your job when moving forward to arrive late in the box at the crucial time to receive a pass, so both speed and timing are essential. You will also be covering a large area of the pitch to help the team with your defensive duties and need good stamina levels as a result.

Wide midfielder

If you play as a winger or wide midfielder, it is likely that you are quick and possess good balance and agility. Speed is a key attribute for a wide midfielder, taking on and beating defenders as well as tracking back to help defensively. This means you are likely to cover a lot of ground in a match so excellent stamina is also necessary to keep going for the full 90 minutes.

Statistic

In the 2002 and 2006 World Cup finals more than 20% of all the goals scored were in the last 15 minutes.

The importance of exercise

Fitness is obviously an important element if you want to play a good standard of football. When you were younger you may not have needed to exercise to keep fit; you naturally used up a lot of energy and kept fit in your daily routines and activities. As you get older, you will notice that you need to work a little harder to keep in good physical condition – and this is where regular exercise fits in.

Exercise is good for you. It helps develop you as a person, both physically and mentally.

Table 2.1 **Exercise benefits**

Physical benefits	Mental benefits
• Improves your posture and body shape. • Helps cardio-vascular fitness – keeping your muscles supplied with oxygen. • Develops your muscle tone and strength. • Strengthens your bones. • Reduces your chance of illness.	• Helps relieve stress and tension. • Increases self-confidence. • Gives you a challenge. • It's fun – gives you something to look forward to!

Genetics plays a part – some people need very little exercise to maintain a high fitness level, while others need a daily physical activity to keep fit. Even though some seem to be born with a head start, this doesn't mean that other less naturally fit people cannot see massive improvements providing they train and work hard. If you stop any physical activity for a while, you will definitely notice the difference with your body and your state of mind. Get to know your body and your fitness levels. At what times do you feel at your best? When do your energy levels feel low? How long does it take you to recover from exercise?

The technical bit . . .

Whenever we exercise our respiratory system responds in obvious ways such as shortness of breath and gasping for air. This is because the body uses more energy as we exercise and our muscles demand more oxygen to maintain this energy level. The fitter we are through regular exercise, the greater our lung capacity and efficiency, and the less we gasp for breath.

Cardiovascular fitness involves keeping oxygen supplied to your muscles from your heart and lungs. Several things happen to your heart while you exercise. Your heart rate (beats per minute) goes up, increasing the speed at which your heart pumps blood and oxygen to your muscles. The stroke volume also increases, which is the amount of blood pumped from the heart during each beat. When you are exercising hard, your heart rate can go up as much as almost three times its resting rate. Well-trained athletes can have a resting rate as low as 30 beats per minute, with most people having a resting heart rate of approximately 60 beats per minute. Lowering the recovery time of your heart rate after exercise to its resting rate is a good sign that you are improving your fitness.

Top tip

Find out how fit you are. Measure your resting heart rate. When you are fully relaxed, find your pulse by placing two fingers over your wrist or the side of your neck and record the number of beats over a minute. Repeat this after some heavy exercise, continuing to measure your heart rate every four or five minutes until you have reached your resting rate. Record the time it took and try it again throughout the season to check if the time increases or decreases.

Statistic

On average a heart beats approximately 86,400 times a day.

A training programme

Your performance as a player can be improved by fitness training. There are five general training categories:

1   Aerobic – endurance training, working your heart and lungs over a long time.

2   Anaerobic – short, quick, powerful activities to build up muscles.

3   Strength – weight training, developing specific muscles.

4   Flexibility – active and passive stretching of muscles.

5   Skills – improving skills and techniques, supporting specific fitness.

Your training programme is likely to be planned and organized by your coach. It needs to suit you, so make sure you talk to your coach, sharing your views. Answer these questions about yourself, as these will influence the type of programme you could have:

How fit are you now?

What exercises do you like?

Do you have any injuries?

What exercises do you dislike?

Do you have any health problems?

Are there any particular aspects you want to work on (speed, strength, stamina, suppleness)?

Your training will vary for each stage of the year:

1   **Pre-season training: aerobic, anaerobic, flexibility and skills training, with some strength training.**

2 Training during the season: maintain level of general fitness and rest after matches.

3 Recuperation: rest and relax at the end of the season to recover from any injuries and fatigue, maintain flexibility.

4 Out-of-season training: aerobic and strength training, maintain flexibility.

It is essential that a coach advises you on any training programme you undertake. They will consider the different fitness components, known as FITT:

Frequency – how often should the type of exercise be performed?
Intensity – how hard should the exercise be?
Time – how long should the exercise session be?
Type – what types of exercises should you use?

With the help of your coach you can develop a weekly programme to support your general and specific fitness. Table 2.2 is an example of the content of a typical pre-season training programme. It is not in any particular order, and does not include warming up and cooling down.

Table 2.2 **Pre-season training program**

Aerobic training	5 × 400 m with 30 seconds recovery or 5–10 km run
Anaerobic training	10 × 20 m shuttle followed by 30 seconds' rest
	10 × 50 m followed by 60 seconds' rest
Strength training	Squat jumps, press-ups, weights/resistance work in a gym
Flexibility training	Careful stretching for each major muscle group
Skills training	Working on specific skills

Summary

- **The four Ss are fundamental components of fitness.**

- **Different playing positions require different physical attributes.**

- **Exercise has both physical and mental benefits.**

- **When you exercise, your heart rate (the number of beats per minute) and your stroke volume (amount of blood in each beat) both increase.**

Self testers

1 What are the four Ss of general fitness?
2 What are the physical requirements of a holding midfielder?
3 Why do we get short of breath when we exercise?

Action plan

Think about a training plan for you for each part of the year. Talk about it with your coach and write it up as a weekly programme. Monitor your fitness each month to check progress.

For more information on fitness, we advise you to read *The Official FA Guide to Fitness for Football* by Dr Richard Hawkins.

Chapter 3

Food for a footballer

THIS CHAPTER WILL:
- Explain the importance of a healthy balanced diet.
- Give an understanding of what to eat and when.
- Examine the place of carbohydrates in a footballer's diet.

Quote | 'You are what you eat.'

This is a well-known phrase that shows the importance of food for our bodies. So what does it mean? It is basically saying that the food you eat has a direct effect on the type of person you are. If you want to lead a healthy lifestyle, stay fit and become physically strong so that you give your best in training and in matches – your diet really does matter.

Nutrients

All living things need food as the basic fuel for living. Food keeps us warm, gives us energy and helps us grow. Our food and drink contain a variety of nutrients, including carbohydrates, fats and proteins. The aim is to try to get the right balance of these each day. Energy-giving foods contain carbohydrates and fats, which are burned up slowly by the body. Energy in food is measured in calories, with a high calorie diet needed if you exercise regularly and burn the calories off. Foods that help us grow and body-building foods are high in protein. Look at Table 3.1 to find out a little more about different food types:

Table 3.1 **Food types**

Nutrient	What does this do?	Where do we get them from?
Carbohydrates	These are mainly stored in muscles, for example, glycogen, used for energy. Great demands are placed on these carbohydrate stores during exercise.	Simple carbohydrates (sugars): sweets, cakes, soft drinks Complex carbohydrates (starches): rice, bread, pasta, potatoes, cereal, fruit.
Fats	These are mainly stored in body tissues and muscles. They help produce energy.	Butter, margarine, oils, oily fish, cheese, whole milk, nuts.
Proteins	These are needed for the growth and repair of body tissues, and to help with the immune system.	Milk, cheese, meat, yoghurt, soya, fish, eggs, nuts.
Vitamins and minerals	These play an important part in being healthy and feeling well.	Present in tiny quantities in natural foods: fruit, vegetables, nuts, fish, meat, eggs, dairy products, cereals.
Fibre	In the digestive system these help absorb and use nutrients.	Wholegrain cereals, fruit, vegetables, seeds, peas, beans.
Water	Performs many functions – essential for healthy living.	Foods, drinks.

A balanced diet

No single food contains all the nutrients we need, so it is important that we eat a wide variety. A balanced diet is one that gives the right mix to keep us healthy and fit. Figure 3.1 shows examples of foods from the main food types, and the proportion recommended to be eaten each day.

Figure 3.1 **The daily recommended requirements of the major food groups**

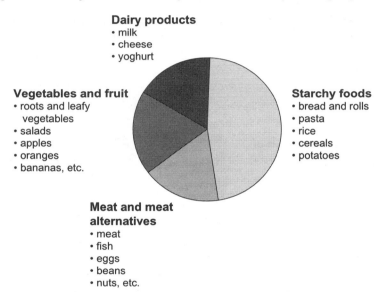

Dairy products
• milk
• cheese
• yoghurt

Vegetables and fruit
• roots and leafy
  vegetables
• salads
• apples
• oranges
• bananas, etc.

Starchy foods
• bread and rolls
• pasta
• rice
• cereals
• potatoes

Meat and meat alternatives
• meat
• fish
• eggs
• beans
• nuts, etc.

The best food for football

Playing any level of football uses energy and will burn off calories. If you play at a competitive level, you can burn off between 600 and 800 calories during a match, so energy-giving food is needed in your diet. This means that it is best to increase the amount of carbohydrates you eat. Make sure they are mainly 'complex' carbohydrates, such as rice, bread, pasta, cereal and fruit, rather than the 'simple' sugary carbohydrates.

Figure 3.2 **The daily recommended requirements of the main nutrients**

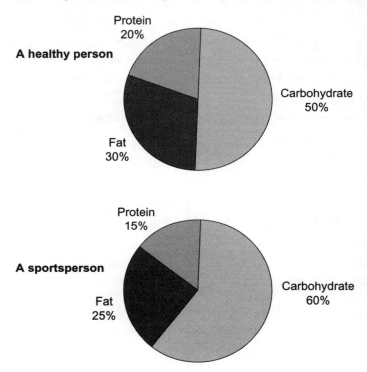

Figure 3.2 shows the difference in diet between a normal healthy person and that recommended for a sportsperson.

It is recommended that active footballers should get as much as 60–70 per cent of their daily diet in the form of carbohydrates. This is because the carbohydrate stores in your body can run out during exercise.

To ensure that your diet is high in carbohydrate and also 'balanced', a mixture of carbohydrate-rich foods and drinks should be consumed. If you have a good variety it will mean that you will take in enough of the other nutrients such as protein, vitamins, minerals and fibre. The following foods are rich in carbohydrates:

- **Breads, pizza bases and crispbreads.**
- **Rice, pasta and noodles.**
- **Potatoes and potato products.**
- **Peas, beans, lentils and corn.**
- **Fruit – fresh, dried and tinned.**
- **Sugar, jam and honey.**
- **Biscuits, cakes and buns.**
- **Muesli bars.**
- **Yoghurts and puddings.**
- **Sports drinks.**

Top tip

When you go shopping for food, think about the types of food you *should* eat. Are there any changes you could make?

You need to eat three meals a day, and even this may not provide enough carbohydrate intake if you are active in sport. Therefore, snacking should play an important role in your nutrition programme. These are popular snacks for footballers as they are high in carbohydrates and relatively low in fat:

- **Jam, honey, banana or peanut butter sandwiches.**
- **Muesli bars, popcorn.**
- **Fruit cake, currant buns, scones.**
- **Crumpets, bagels, muffins.**
- **Cereal, rice pudding.**

▨ Think about the food you eat and the types of snacks you have. Could you alter the types of food you eat? Decide the best times for you to eat snacks. Some footballers like to eat and drink straight after exercise, some like to have a drink and wait an hour or two before eating a snack or meal.

> ### Top tip
> Keep up your carbohydrate levels by eating sensibly at meal times and snacking sensibly throughout the day.

Drinking fluids

During training and when playing matches it is vital to drink regularly to maintain hydration. Feeling thirsty is a sign of being dehydrated, but then it is a little late – by the time you are thirsty you are already partly dehydrated. If you finish a training session and you are thirsty, then you have not taken enough fluid on board during the session. Whenever you become thirsty start to drink immediately. Preferably, drink before you are thirsty. However, try not to drink too much in one go during a match or training. Drinking too much, too quickly, particularly if already dehydrated, can cause stomach upset.

Drinking plain water is not the most effective way to rehydrate as drinks should contain moderate electrolyte levels (sodium and some potassium). Sports drinks are a good choice as they are specially made with the correct mix of carbohydrates, fluid and electrolytes.

> ### Top tip
> Maintain fluid levels throughout the day by drinking little and often.

Summary

- **Nutrition has an important effect on your overall performance as a footballer.**

- **A balanced diet will ensure you take in enough nutrients to keep you healthy and fit.**

- **Carbohydrate-rich foods need to be eaten to maintain high energy levels while playing matches and training.**

- **Drink enough fluid to stay hydrated.**

Self testers

1 Name five foods that are high in carbohydrates.

2 Approximately what percentage of the daily diet of a footballer should be carbohydrates?

3 Drinking a lot of water in one go during exercise is the best way to rehydrate. True or false?

Action plan

List the types of food you eat in a week. Check the list against the foods recommended for a balanced diet and one that is rich in carbohydrates (see Figures 3.1 and 3.2). If you need to alter your diet consider the types of snacks you should eat, and when you should eat them, as well as eating well for the three main meals of the day.

For more information on nutrition, we advise you to read *The Official FA Guide to Fitness for Football* by Dr Richard Hawkins.

Chapter 4

Choosing your kit

THIS CHAPTER WILL:
- Explain the importance of wearing kit that is appropriate for different conditions.
- Give advice on boot maintenance.
- Give guidance on useful equipment to have for training and playing football.

Football kits

There has been incredible change in the style and manufacture of football kits in the past 60 years. Compared to the heavy, baggy kit of the 1950s, tops and shorts are now lightweight, breathable and very practical. The invention of synthetic fibres, such as nylon, acrylic and polyester, made a big difference in this respect. Today, kits are constantly changing, largely due to commercial influences on the game.

Statistic

Players often wore caps, and sometimes even top hats, for matches in the nineteenth century!

The choice of football kit is, obviously, down to you. The main consideration is comfort and fit. Make sure that the shorts and top aren't too tight, and wear appropriate layers of clothes for the weather conditions. It is important that you are warm enough in cold weather and cool enough in hot weather, and wearing a few thin layers for training is a good way to regulate your temperature. You must also have layers of clothing, such as a tracksuit and waterproofs, to put on if you are a substitute or are substituted during a match. Sudden changes in body temperature once you stop being active need to be regulated by putting on extra layers for warmth. Also remember that, if it is hot weather, dark tops absorb the heat and make you feel hotter.

Football socks are important items to get right. Make sure you choose the correct size, wash them regularly, and check that they have no rough areas next to your feet. A poor pair of socks could cause you unnecessary foot injuries severe enough to stop you playing for a few weeks. If your socks cause problems, then change them for a new pair.

Top tip
If you are find that socks cause problems for your feet, wear a thin pair of cotton socks beneath the football socks.

Football boots
Colour, make, price and style are probably your main reasons for choosing a particular pair of boots. Try to ask yourself a few more questions about the boots before making your selection:

- **Are the football boots comfortable?**
- **Do the boots fit well, especially in the width, with football socks?**

- Are the boots flexible in all directions, including the bottom of the boot?
- Do the boots provide enough protection and support?

Choose your boots wisely and try them on before buying. One difficult decision you need to make concerns the type of studs to use: screw-in, moulded or blades. The main consideration is the condition and type of surface you will be playing on:

Condition of playing surface	Usual types of studs
Soft ground	Screw-in or blades
Firm ground	Moulded or short blades
Hard ground	Rubber studs or AstroTurf™

Screw-in studs

Advantages

- Studs can be changed if they get worn down, so boots last longer.
- Long and short studs are available for some boots, so they can be changed to match the conditions of the pitch.
- Screw-in studs give excellent grip on soft ground, enabling you to turn, sprint and stop confidently.
- They are a popular type of boot, so there is plenty of choice of style and brand.

Disadvantages

- There are usually fewer studs than on moulded boots so pressure points and blisters can occur if they are used on hard pitches.
- If you don't regularly check and tighten the studs you can lose them while playing. Even worse, playing with a loose stud can wear out the screw-thread on the boot so that it can never tighten.

Screw-in studs

Top tip

Put a little grease or lubricant on the screw to ensure the screw/stud does not rust in place.

Moulded studs

Advantages

- Moulded boots usually have a large number of studs, so the pressure is more evenly distributed on your foot. This minimizes the chance of blisters.

- The studs are shorter than screw-in studs, making them more suitable for firm pitches with grip on the top surface.

- Astro Turf™ boots are moulded with pimples or small blades and are excellent for artificial grass on training grounds. They are not suitable for grass unless the ground is very hard.

- The football season is getting longer with tournaments and footy camps throughout the year. This means that you are likely to play on harder pitches during the summer months.

Disadvantages

- The studs are usually rubber or nylon, and once they are worn down the boots need replacing.

- On wet surfaces or soft ground they provide very poor grip and will definitely affect your performance.

Blades

Advantages

- There has been a lot of research into the new designs of bladed boots. They claim to provide better turning speed and grip.

- The design means they may be less likely to get stuck in the ground when running.

- Some boots have short and long blades available for different pitch conditions.

- Some blades have replaceable tips so that they can be changed if they become worn or damaged.

Disadvantages

- If you change from traditional studs to blades they may take a little getting used to as the turning motion is different and does not suit all players.

Blades

Statistic

Remember, you will probably run about 8 km during a game of football so your boots are important!

Uppers

The top of your boots, or uppers, could be leather or synthetic. In some cases the upper will consist of a mixture of the two. Leather can fit comfortably to the shape of the foot, with a good feel to the ball. However, leather can also stretch when wet and go out of shape. Synthetic boots are generally cheaper than leather but have improved in recent years. Many now have the ability to let the foot breathe, reducing sweating and making the boot more comfortable to wear. Synthetic uppers are also often used to make a lighter boot.

Choose the boot that is good for you, remembering that comfort is important and so is ball control. The position of laces now varies, from the traditional top of the foot position to running down the side of the boot. When you try on football boots, decide whether you want the laces off centre so that the laces do not get in the way when you strike a ball. Do the boots have a padded tongue that is used to hide the laces, providing a flat surface to strike the ball with? Does the tongue move about or is it secured with velcro or a strap?

Also think about the protection that the boot gives your foot. Some lighter boots may offer less protection for the foot but are ideal for fast running as a winger or striker. Other boots may offer good protection but are heavier and may be more suited to defenders, goalkeepers or midfielders.

Looking after your boots

Here are a few tips to keep your boots in good condition. Remember that your boots should not only look good, but also feel good!

- Undo the laces properly when you take your boots off.
- Remove soil by banging the boots together or using a brush, then wipe them with a damp cloth.
- If wet, allow the football boots to dry before polishing them or giving them a final clean. Don't dry your boots near a fire or radiator in case the boots crack or lose their shape.
- Stuffing leather boots with newspaper helps them retain their shape and will help draw any moisture from inside the boot.
- Don't play in boots with loose studs, broken studs, mixed studs, or over-tightened studs.

- Don't keep boots in a plastic bag.
- Put your boots on in the dressing room or at the side of the pitch. Walking across car parks or on concrete paths will damage the soles and sharpen the studs or blades.
- Check the boots on a regular basis, looking for any cracks or damage and tightening the studs if necessary.

Equipment list

Make sure you check your bag before you leave for any practices or matches. Here's a checklist of the items you may need to take with you:

- ❑ Kit – shorts, top and socks
- ❑ Thin inner socks
- ❑ Warm-up top/bottoms
- ❑ Boots (moulded) for firm ground
- ❑ Boots (screw-in/blades) for soft ground
- ❑ Boot bag for muddy boots
- ❑ Shin pads
- ❑ Stud key
- ❑ Extra pair of laces
- ❑ Extra studs for replacements
- ❑ Tape or tie-ups for socks
- ❑ Towel and shower gel (if shower available)
- ❑ Bottle of water/drink
- ❑ First-aid kit – plasters, elasticated bandage, muscle spray, etc.
- ❑ Small bag for valuables

For practising the drills in Chapters 8 and 9, equipment lists are provided for each drill. You will generally need a size 5 ball and a supply of, say, eight cones to mark off boundaries for your practice grids.

Summary

- Wear kit to suit the weather conditions.

- A good boot should give you support, stability, grip and traction.

- Choose studs or blades to match the condition of the pitch – use screw-in or blades for a soft pitch and moulded or short blades for firm pitches.

- Keep your boots in good condition to prolong their life.

- Always be prepared for a match, checking your kit is ready and packed to go.

Self testers

1   Why are dark tops not so good in hot weather?
2   Which types of studs are better for soft ground?
3   Give two advantages of wearing moulded studs.

Action plan

1   Check the equipment list (p.56) and make sure you have all you need for training and for matches.
2   Find a suitable box or bag to store all the (clean!) equipment so that you are always organized and prepared each time you play football.

Chapter 5

Warming up and cooling down

> THIS CHAPTER WILL:
> - Explain the importance of warming up before a match and at the start of training.
> - Give an understanding of the importance of cooling down.
> - Describe ways to stretch different muscles.

If you go to watch any professional football team playing a match, it is well worth getting to the stadium early to watch the players warming up and stretching. Most teams are out on the pitch 45 minutes before the match carrying out exercise routines and stretches under the watchful eye of the coach. This is quite a contrast to some local league teams, with players turning up ten minutes before a match and using the run from the changing room to the pitch as their warm-up. Obviously these are two extremes, but this chapter will help to show the importance of a good warm-up and cool-down before and after a match, and even during half-time.

The warm-up

The warm-up is designed to prepare a player for any physical activity, both at training and for a match. Your body needs gradual 'waking up' from a resting state to a state of readiness to train or play. It is important that the warm-up is gradual, building up from easy walking, movement of joints and jogging, through to sprinting and quick turning. Ideally you want a warm-up to match your movements in a game so that similar muscles and joints are prepared for action. In the warm-up, use exercises such as side-strides, sharp turns and jumping, as well as ball control and passing. These exercises will not only prepare muscles and joints, but will also have the advantage of ensuring the effect is on those muscles used for playing football, helping prevent injuries. Warming up with a football 'tunes you in' to football skills, preparing you mentally for the game, and gives you the chance get a feel for the playing surface.

Statistic

The recommended time for warming up is between 15 and 25 minutes, completing the warm-up approximately 5–10 minutes before a match.

The main purposes for warming up are to:

- raise body temperature
- increase muscle temperature
- reduce muscle tightness
- help achieve joint mobility
- prepare the cardiovascular and respiratory systems
- decrease the risk of injury
- prepare mentally for physical activity.

The technical bit

The term 'warm-up' implies the key objective of raising body and muscle temperature. As muscles contract they use up energy. Less than a quarter of this energy goes towards producing mechanical work, with the rest of the energy generating heat within the muscle cells. By moving muscles, their performance is improved as their temperature rises. However, this is only one part of improving their performance: raising body temperature by just 1° C is enough to maximize the effect on the active muscles. It has been found that the best way to generate the necessary internal heat is by running.

Mobility and flexibility

Warming up helps you keep mobile and flexible through moving your joints and stretching.

- **Mobility is the amount of movement your joints will allow.**
- **Flexibility is the amount of 'stretch' your muscles allow as you move.**

Flexibility exercises increase the stretching potential of the muscles, improving movement. Daily stretching is important, so use the examples on the following pages to work out a routine.

Good mobility is essential for sprinting, turning, tackling and shooting. Before any sudden twisting or explosive movements, you need to move your joints in a slow smooth action. Preparing your back and neck is particularly important before any exercise.

Joint rotations

From a balanced, standing position with your arms hanging loosely at your sides, bend, extend, and rotate each of the following joints. Perform eight to ten rotations for each group of joints before moving on to the next group:

- **Fingers**
- **Wrists**
- **Elbows**
- **Neck**
- **Back and shoulder blades**
- **Hips**
- **Knees**
- **Ankles**
- **Feet and toes.**

Work through this sequence of rotations slowly and smoothly, and think about the movements that occur at each joint. Complete the series of joint rotations from fingers to toes in no more than three to four minutes.

Statistic

You begin to lose natural mobility and flexibility from eight years old, so all players need to know how to work on muscles and joints.

Stretching

Correct stretching of your muscles each day, and before training and matches, is important to help avoid injuries and to improve flexibility and performance. Stretching is quite 'static' so it needs to form part of an active warm-up. Common sense and some thought is needed to make the stretching effective:

- Don't overstretch or put too much strain on your muscles. If there is any pain, stop and find a different position. Stretching shouldn't be painful; just hold a stretch up to a point of tension.

- Don't stretch if your muscles are very cold – warm them up first and also get your joints mobile by rotating and moving wrists, hips, knees, etc.

- Start with very gentle stretching, and make each movement slow. Hold a stretch for 10–15 seconds and slowly release, repeating several times.

- Don't 'bounce' into a stretch – you need to control the movement.

- Be systematic so you don't miss out any particular muscle group.

Top tip

Try to develop a daily stretching routine. Spend a few minutes in the morning gently stretching key muscles – it will increase your flexibility and help avoid injuries. Animals such as cats and dogs enjoy a good stretch after waking up, and look at their flexibility!

▓ Try the following stretches for the major muscle groups of the body.

Figure 5.1 **Major muscle groups**

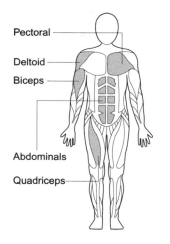

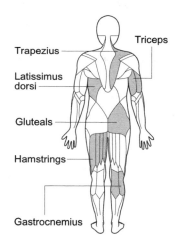

Calf stretch

Facing a wall or partner, step forwards onto a bent left leg, with your hands on the wall or on your partner. Increasing the weight on your hands, deepen the left leg bend and straighten your right leg back. You should feel the stretch at the top of the calf on the right leg. Try to make the heel of your right leg touch the ground but don't force it. Hold it for ten seconds and repeat three or four times for each leg.

Figure 5.2 **Calf stretch**

Quads stretch

Stand to the side of a wall or partner for balance. Gently raise one heel up behind you by grasping the ankle with your hand. Feel the stretch in the quadriceps just above the knees. Repeat with the other leg.

Figure 5.3 **Quads stretch**

Hamstring stretch – standing

Straighten one leg in front of you and slightly bend back the other leg. Place both hands on the thigh of your bent leg and sit back gently. Don't bounce, hold it for 10–15 seconds and then change legs.

Figure 5.4 **Hamstring stretch – standing**

Hamstring stretch – lying down

Lie on your back with your legs out flat. With your hands holding behind your left knee, raise your leg at the hip, with the knee still bent at 90°. Hold this position and then slowly raise your leg at the knee joint until a stretch can be felt in the hamstring muscles. Relax and repeat three or four times for each leg.

Figure 5.5 **Hamstring stretch – lying down**

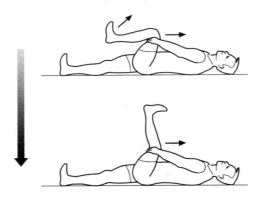

Gluteal stretch

Sit on the ground with knees pointing skywards. Cross your left leg over your right so it is resting behind the knee. Gently push the crossed leg towards your chest with the help of the other leg. Don't push too far and repeat for the other leg.

Figure 5.6 **Gluteal stretch**

Groin inward stretch

Sit on the floor with your knees bent and lean back on your hands. Slowly push one leg in and downward until you feel a little strain on your thigh. Hold it for five to ten seconds, release and repeat four times on each leg.

Figure 5.7 **Groin inward stretch**

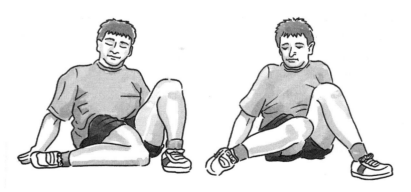

Groin outward stretch

Stand with legs wide apart and weight even, knees slightly bent and hands on hips. Increase the bend in one leg and straighten the other by sliding it out so you take a sideways lunge. Don't bounce, and the knee of the bent leg should not go beyond the foot position.

Figure 5.8 **Groin outward stretch**

Back stretch

Lie on your back and bring in your hips and knees until your knees touch your chest. Put your hands on your knees and gently pull them towards your chest, lifting your hips slightly. Lift your head carefully and slowly off the ground until you feel a slight stretch in your back.

Figure 5.9 **Back stretch**

Side stretch

Stand upright and balanced. Reach your left hand up and over your head, bending slowly to your right. Slide your right hand down your right leg as you bend. Keep your hips still and weight evenly balanced as you bend. Don't bounce, and repeat this stretch for the other side.

Figure 5.10 **Side stretch**

Stomach stretch

Lie on your back with your arms stretched up over your head on the ground. Stretch as far as you can with your toes pointed forwards and fingers reaching back. Hold the stretch for 30 seconds.

Figure 5.11 **Stomach stretch**

Fast feet and speed

Speed is crucial in football, whether it's for a quick, heart-pumping 5-m sprint, or a lung-gasping 50-m break. In a race for the ball between a defender and a striker, pace makes all the difference between winning and losing possession. This is why most teams include some 'fast feet' and speed drills in the warm-up. They tune you in for the match, improving coordination and speed, and preparing your brain and nerves for the fast movements to come in the match.

▨ As part of your warm-up, try to include five to ten minutes of drills involving quick foot movement and sprinting over small distances. Try the following drills and make up some of your own.

On the spot

Jog on the spot and then sprint hard on the spot, pumping your arms for five seconds. Relax into a jog and repeat. Continue this, varying the quick feet movement:

- **Move in a 'figure of eight on the spot.**
- **Sprint and end with a header.**
- **Sprint with knees up.**

Taps

Place two footballs 10 m apart. Sprint from one football to the other. When you reach a football, hop quickly from foot to foot, tapping the top of the ball with alternate feet. Repeat this for ten sprints. Vary the action at each football:

- **Pass the ball quickly from side to side.**
- **Bend the leg and touch the top of the ball with alternate knees.**

Zig-zag

Set up two rows of five cones, hurdles, footballs or any markers, about 3 m apart. Run to the first marker on the right-hand side and place your right foot over it. Push off from this foot and accelerate across to the first marker on the left row. Continue with the zig-zag pathway, moving sideways quickly and pushing off to change direction.

Shuttles

Place four markers in a row, each 3 m apart. Make a start line, 3 m in front of the first marker. Sprint to each marker in any order, touching them with one hand and returning to the start line each time.

A warm-up programme

Before each match and at the start of training, your coach is likely to plan a 15–20 minute programme for warming up, which includes stretching. It is always a good idea to stretch once your muscles have warmed up a little, after an initial jog. Table 5.1 on p. 74 shows an outline of a programme that can be adapted for your use before a match.

Cooling down

Cooling or warming down is seen as essential in many other sports such as athletics, swimming and cycling, but it is only in recent years that it has become part of the routine after football matches. It is often easier to fit in a cool-down (warm-down) after training than after a match because all the players are still wound up in the emotions of the game they have just played. However, cooling down after a match should be part of your routine if you want to look after your body.

Table 5.1 **Warm-up programme**

Activities	Duration/Distance
1 Jog – very easy pace across pitch and back twice.	4 × 50 m
2 Joint rotations – slow circular movement of all joints: ankles, knees, hips, wrists, elbows, shoulders. Gentle neck and back movement.	3 minutes
3 Jog – cruising pace across pitch and back twice: • Normal run. • Side-strides. • Backwards during run. • Cross-steps during run.	4 × 50 m
4 Stretching – light stretching (quads, hamstrings, groin, back) and include specific stretches you need.	5 minutes
5 Fast feet drills – on the spot.	2 minutes
6 Speed drills – 10-m course: • Run 3 m, decelerate to end, then run hard back – short strides. • Sideways run along start line then sprint forward 10 m. • Jump twice at start then sprint forward 10 m.	3 minutes
7 Ball work in pairs – 15–25 ball touches per player each minute.	5 minutes

The most important thing is that a cool-down is active but gentle. You are aiming to gradually return your heart rate and respiration back to normal, and to allow the waste products (lactic acid) from the muscles to be reabsorbed. If you cool down too quickly at the end of a match or training, particularly if you have been working very hard, you are more likely to suffer from muscle stiffness caused by a build-up of lactic acid. Figure 5.12 on page 76 shows the importance of an active cool-down.

Cooling down helps prevent muscle stiffness.

Immediately after a match, take a few minutes' rest. Your coach may wish to talk to you and this is when you will share the experience of the match with your team-mates. It is important that you take in fluids to start rehydration at this stage. The best form of cool-down is jogging, at an easy pace for several minutes, going down to a walk. Ten minutes' cool-down is enough to have a positive effect.

Gentle stretching can also be part of the cool-down. It helps bring your body back towards a state of rest and recovery and allows you to focus on relaxing and lengthening the muscles that you have put under stress during the match or training.

Figure 5.12 **Levels of lactic acid after activity (Bangsbo1994)**
Source: *Fitness Training in Football – A Scientific Approach*, Jens Bangsbo (Ho & Storm) (1994)

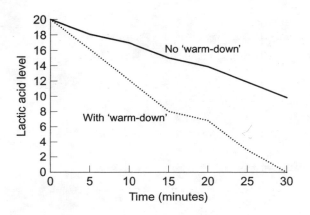

Top tip

Cool down after each match or training with a gentle jog and stretch. Not only will it ease any muscle aches, but it has also been shown to improve your sleep in the immediate nights that follow.

Summary

- Warming up and cooling down need to be part of your routine before and after matches and training.

- Stretching is important to maximize performance and reduce the risk of injury.

- Make stretching and joint movement part of a daily routine.

Self testers

1 Give three reasons for warming up before a match.

2 Describe a stretch for your hamstring.

3 Why are 'fast feet' exercises useful as part of the warm-up before a match?

Action plan

1 Plan a warm-up routine for yourself before a match or training. Think about a balance of exercises for the different parts of your body.

2 Get into the habit of stretching muscles and moving joints as a routine each day.

For more information on warming up and cooling down, we advise you to read *The Official FA Guide to Fitness for Football* by Dr Richard Hawkins.

Chapter 6

Dealing with injuries

THIS CHAPTER WILL:
- Describe the different sorts of injuries that you may be unlucky enough to sustain as a footballer.
- Outline ways to help you prevent injuries.
- Explain the basic treatments that are needed for different injuries.

Football is a high-energy, body-contact sport, so at some stage in your football career you will get an injury. Don't let this put you off, though! The more informed you are about the different types of possible injuries and the way to avoid and treat injuries, the more chance you have of getting through each season with fewer injury problems.

Statistic
A total of more than 3,000 injuries are suffered each season by the 2,500 or so professionals in the Premier League and Football League. Each injury keeps a player out for an average of four matches.

The information in this chapter is for guidance and general interest. If you are concerned about any injuries you have, and certainly if the injury is serious, you must seek medical advice from your doctor or visit a hospital.

Types of injury

There are two different types of sporting injury – **chronic** and **acute** injuries. The causes for these make each distinctive.

Chronic injuries

These are caused by continuous stress on a particular part of the body over a long period of time. Examples for other sports include tennis elbow or golfer's elbow. There are fewer chronic injuries involved with football, but if you overuse a particular part of the body for too long you may get a chronic injury. A possible problem if you run long distances in training is an injury called 'shin splints'. Symptoms include:

- **tenderness on the inside of the shin**
- **lower leg pain**
- **possible swelling**
- **pain when the foot is bent downwards**
- **a slight redness to the shin.**

If you suffer from this, the main thing to do is rest. You can apply ice in the early stages when it is very painful, but the sooner you rest the sooner it will heal. To prevent chronic injuries, train carefully, rest between training sessions, wear good footwear and improve your technique.

Acute injuries

These are caused by a sudden stress on the body and in football are more common than chronic injuries. They can include bone fractures, pulled muscles, concussion or bruising. It is useful to separate these types of injuries into **soft tissue** and **hard tissue** injuries.

Soft tissue

- Open injuries where the skin is broken, such as cuts, grazes and blisters.

- Closed injuries that happen beneath the skin:
  - bruises – blood vessels get damaged
  - strains – pulled muscles and tendons from torn tissue
  - sprains – ligaments stretched or torn at a joint such as an ankle
  - dislocation – bone pulled out of its normal position at a joint
  - torn cartilage – damage to the cartilage around a joint such as the knee.

Statistic

The largest single type of injury in football, by a long way, is a muscle strain. This accounts for about one-third of all injuries.

Hard tissue

These injuries are **bone fractures**. They could be cracks in the bone, or an actual break. With a fractured bone there is likely to be bruising and swelling, as well as a great deal of pain because of the damaged nerves inside the bone.

Treating injuries

The majority of the injuries you will sustain playing football will be minor soft tissue injuries such as sprains, strains and bruises. The **RICE** method is a good way to treat these:

R   REST   → Stop immediately and rest the injury.

I   ICE   → Apply ice to the injury to make the blood vessels contract and reduce swelling.

C   COMPRESSION   → Put on a bandage (not too tight) to help reduce swelling.

E   ELEVATION   → Raise the injury to reduce the flow of blood.

Anything more serious than a minor soft tissue injury will need proper medical attention. This includes any fracture, dislocation or torn cartilage, or any injury to the head.

Looking after your feet

Feet are obviously a key part of the body when playing football, and yet foot-care advice is largely ignored by many footballers. Infections and painful problems can result if simple advice isn't followed, possibly preventing you from training and playing.

Blisters

Blisters are layers of the outer surface of the skin separated from one another, caused by twisting or friction on the foot. The empty space between the separated skin layers is often filled with fluid. If this fluid contains blood, this signifies a deeper blister that will need treatment to stop infection.

Prevention

- Ensure correctly fitting footwear.
- Introduce the wearing of new footwear slowly.
- Wet and stretch areas of footwear that may cause friction.
- Wear thin cotton socks, perhaps sweat-absorbent, under football socks.
- Try applying Vaseline™ or other similar 'second skins' on areas of the foot liable to friction.

Treatment

- Clean the area with antiseptic cream or lotion.
- Apply cotton-backed tape and a large foam pad over the area, with a hole cut to the size of the blister.

Calluses

These are caused by excessive friction and pressure, resulting in a thickening of the skin. They are tender and painful to touch.

Prevention

- Ensure correctly fitting footwear.
- Wear thin cotton socks, perhaps sweat-absorbent, under football socks.
- There could be a problem with the alignment of your foot, so see a doctor or podiatrist.

Treatment

- Calluses can be trimmed by a podiatrist or chiropodist to relieve the pressure.
- Change footwear to give a better fit.
- Foot alignment may be altered if this is diagnosed as the problem.

Athlete's foot

This is caused by a fungus and can spread very quickly. This is particularly the case if players walk around barefoot in changing rooms with contaminated floors. It commonly occurs between the toes, with white scaly skin, usually itchy and burning.

Prevention

* Wear flip-flops in the changing room and shower area.
* Use footbaths.
* Dry between your toes after washing, applying powder if necessary.
* Don't share towels or socks with other players.

Treatment

* Consult a doctor or pharmacist.
* Use the prescribed anti-fungal cream, lotion or powder regularly until the infection goes.
* Keep the toes clean, dry and out in the air during this period.

Ingrowing toenails

Problems may occur if you cut your nails too short, or cut down into each corner. This may cause a red swelling of the skin and a discharge from the nail bed around the edge of the nail. In extreme cases, you may get an ingrowing toenail, when the nail, or a ragged nail spike, grows down into the skin at the side of the nail.

Prevention

* Ensure correctly fitting footwear.
* Keep your nails cut even and short, but not too short.
* Don't cut down into the corners of your nail.
* Use a file to smooth the edges of the nail.

Treatment

- If the area around the nail is painful, inflamed and red or has a discharge of fluid, then consult a doctor, podiatrist or chiropodist.

> **Top tip**
>
> One of the main causes of foot problems, including ingrowing toenails, blisters and calluses, are badly fitted shoes, boots or trainers. Choose your footwear carefully and for comfort, not brand, making sure that they are not too tight or too loose.

Cramp and stitch

Cramp

Some people suffer with this more than others, but if you've ever had cramp during a match you'll know it is very painful and makes it almost impossible to continue playing. Your muscle contracts or spasms, with a feeling as if it has 'locked up'. Fortunately it usually goes off after a while, but if you suffer with cramp consistently it may be a good idea to consult your doctor about it. The cause is still partly unknown and based on different theories. It is probably caused by a number of factors:

- Dehydration.
- Overheating.
- Lack of blood flowing to muscles.
- Lack of salt minerals in the blood.
- A build-up of lactic acid in muscles.

Prevention

- Drink plenty of fluids.
- Eat a diet that is suitable for a footballer (see p. 43).
- Warm up and stretch well before the match (see p. 60).
- Rehydrate with fluid at half-time.

Treatment

- Take weight off the affected muscle.
- Carefully stretch the muscle and hold it in a stretched position.
- Massage the muscle gently to relax it and get the blood flowing.
- Drink an isotonic drink to make up for the salt mineral loss.

Stitch

Stitches are likely to be caused by a muscle cramp of the diaphragm – the muscle that helps us breathe. When we inhale (breathe in) we move the diaphragm down, when we exhale (breathe out) it moves up. The diaphragm is positioned between the chest cavity and the abdominal cavity, with the internal organs in the abdomen connected to the diaphragm. During running these organs are bounced around and pull down on the diaphragm as we exhale, causing a stitch. Interestingly most people get a stitch on the right side which is where the largest organ, the liver, is located.

Prevention

- Breathe deeply when running.
- Try to relax your chest and stomach.

Treatment

- Stop exercising for a short while.
- Take deep breaths.
- Breathe out slowly.

Top tip

If you get a stitch while running, try breathing out as your left foot hits the ground. The organs on your left side are smaller than on the right side so this may reduce the effect of a stitch.

Preventing injuries

Many minor injuries sustained during a football match or training can be avoided. This is particularly true for foot problems.

Before the game

- Check your feet are in good condition, with nails cut and any blisters or other problems treated.
- Take off watches, jewellery, etc.
- Check that the area you're practising or playing on is free from glass and stones.
- Warm up correctly, preparing your muscles and joints (see p. 60).

During the game

- Use the correct technique for passing, tackling, heading and shooting.
- Wear comfortable, well-fitting trainers or boots.
- Wear a thin pair of cotton socks under your football socks.
- Check that the stud length suits the condition of the pitch.
- Use a good pair of shin pads.

After the game

- Cool down properly (see p. 73).
- Rest properly to give yourself good recovery time before playing again.

Statistic

Approximately one-third of injuries are sustained during training, while the remaining two-thirds occur during matches.

Summary

* Chronic injuries are caused by overuse over time. Acute injuries are more common and are caused by sudden stress.

* Most acute injuries in football are minor soft tissue injuries such as bruising, strains and sprains. Hard tissue injuries are bone fractures.

* The **RICE** method is a good way to treat minor soft tissue injuries.

* Look after your feet!

* Try to prevent injuries and problems before they occur.

Self testers

1   Give an example of a chronic sporting injury.
2   What does RICE stand for?
3   What are the best ways to prevent blisters?
4   Describe the probable cause of a stitch.

Action plan

List the injuries and problems, however minor, that you have had in the past few years through playing football. For each injury write down possible ways these could have been avoided. Use this to give yourself a checklist of things to do to help prevent or limit injuries in the future.

Part 3

Improving your game

Chapter 7

Football fundamentals

> THIS CHAPTER WILL:
> * Outline some of the basic skills required by all young footballers, irrespective of what position they are playing in.
> * Give technique tips that will help players understand the basic skills.

There are certain basic skills that all footballers need to develop and practise. Football is a team game, with passing the ball an essential part of keeping the ball and developing attacking play. All players need to pass the ball competently and confidently. Controlling the ball from a pass is another basic skill that can be practised. Having a good first touch when receiving the ball looks an effortless skill from top professionals, but it requires excellent technique and great concentration. Other basic skills needed by all players include tackling, shooting and running with the ball. You, as a midfielder, need to practise the techniques needed for these skills to help you become a good all-round team player.

Passing

Passing is the most frequently used technique in the game of football. Coaches will often say 'If you can't pass the ball, you can't play' which is why passing is one of football's fundamentals. Without the ability to pass the ball accurately and precisely, your team will struggle to keep possession and build up attempts on goal.

Passing is one of football's fundamental skills.

A good player will have a wide range of passing techniques, using different parts of the foot surface, which are:

- the inside of the foot
- the outside of the foot
- the instep of the foot
- the toe
- the sole of the foot
- the heel of the foot.

You will also need to consider the different passing options:

- **Do you need to make a short pass?**
- **Does the ball need to travel a long distance?**
- **Do you want to pass in the air or on the ground?**

These decisions help you choose the type of pass to make. You also need to consider the following important elements:

- **Whether to disguise the pass.**
- **Speed or weight of the pass.**
- **Timing of the pass.**
- **Accuracy of the pass.**

When players can effectively and regularly deliver on these elements, they will be considered a good passer of the ball for their team.

Top tip

A good pass is one that arrives just in front of the receiver so they can take the ball without breaking stride and move up field to build their team's attempt on goal – which is an attacking principle of play and the main objective of being in possession.

Although there is a variety of passing techniques that you can practise, this section considers three of the most common passes used in the modern game:

1 **The push pass.**
2 **The low driven pass.**
3 **The lofted pass.**

The push pass

The push pass is the most commonly used pass at all levels of football. For passes up to approximately 25 m, the push pass is also the most accurate.

A push pass

The technique

You should approach the ball at a slight angle with your non-kicking foot placed alongside the ball. Be careful not to get too close as this will prevent you from swinging your kicking leg freely. The ankle of the passing foot should be kept firm. The ball is then passed using the inside of your kicking foot, making contact through the middle of the ball. For accuracy you should follow through in the same direction as the target of the pass. At all times, the head remains steady with eyes fixed on the ball.

The low driven pass

A common pass for footballers to master is the low driven pass. It allows players to pass the ball over longer distances and also at a greater pace, so that the ball reaches the receiver in a shorter period of time.

A low driven pass

The technique

The technique is similar to the push pass, but with modifications at the point of striking the ball. You should approach the ball at a slight angle with your non-kicking foot placed alongside the ball. For this pass, however, the standing foot needs to be slightly in front of the ball. Be careful not to get too close, as this will prevent you from swinging your kicking foot freely through the ball. Your passing foot ankle should be firm. The ball is then passed with the kicking foot making contact through the middle of the ball. The kicking foot needs to fully extend down so that the pass is made using the laces (the instep) of the boot. Once again, the follow through is important and should follow the line of the intended target. At all times the head remains steady, with eyes fixed on the ball.

The lofted pass

When players are choosing their passing options, one thing they will need to consider is whether to pass the ball on the ground or in the air. If

A lofted pass

the opposition have players in between the passer and the team-mate being passed to, then one option is to try the lofted pass. This would take the ball over the head of the defending player and hopefully into the path of the attacker.

The technique

You approach the ball at a slight angle and plant your standing foot alongside the ball, but this time slightly behind the ball. Your last stride into the ball will be longer than previous strides. This allows for you to increase the length of the back swing on your kicking foot. You must not plant your standing foot too close to the ball or it will interfere with swinging your kicking leg freely. Similar to the low driven pass, the point of contact with the ball is made through the laces (the instep) of the boot. However, with this particular pass the contact is made with the underside of the ball. Although it is still important to keep the head steady with eyes fixed on the ball, the body position is slightly leaning back. The length of the back swing of the kicking foot and the pace of the follow through increases the distance of the pass. For accuracy it is important that the follow through is in line with the intended target.

> **Top tip**
>
> Remember to practise your techniques using both feet, not just the foot you prefer.

Ball control

If you watch top players you will soon notice how comfortable they are receiving the ball. They are not worried at all about receiving the ball, just what they are going to do next. Ball control is another football fundamental and something all good players will have spent hours practising on the training ground. You can gain or lose vital seconds depending on how good you are at controlling the ball. As soon as the ball is under control, players quickly consider what to do next. Do they:

- **Look to run with the ball?**
- **Look to dribble?**
- **Try to shoot?**
- **Try to pass the ball to a team-mate? (This is the most common option.)**

So you need to practise getting the ball quickly under control so that you can keep possession of the ball for your team and develop the attacking play. There are four surfaces of the body that you can use to control the ball:

1 The feet.
2 The thigh.
3 The chest.
4 The head.

Controlling the ball

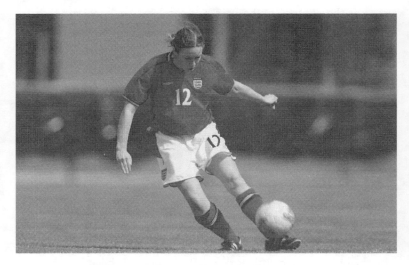

For the purposes of this chapter, we will concentrate on the basic techniques for controlling the ball with the feet, thigh and chest.

> ## Top tip
>
> Players should look to play their first touch away from their body and into a position that will allow them to immediately consider their options – run with ball, dribble, shoot or pass on their second touch.

Whatever surface is chosen to control the ball, there are real advantages of playing the ball out and in front of the body with the first touch.

- **You will gain time to consider options, as the ball is not stuck under the foot.**
- **You will improve your vision for passing/shooting options as your head is likely to be up.**

- Your accuracy will be improved as a vital gap is created between your feet and the ball to help effective technique.

There are two basic types of ball control: the **cushion control** and the **wedge control**. Both can be used by all the different surfaces, though the techniques in this chapter concentrate on the following:

- Cushion control using the inside of the foot.
- Cushion control using the top of the foot.
- Cushion control using the thigh.
- Cushion control using the chest.
- Wedge control using the feet.

Cushion control using the inside of the foot

The technique

It is important to be well balanced when you are receiving the ball, so you must move into the line of the ball as early as possible. This gives you less chance of being caught off balance. Decide which foot you will be

Ball control using the inside of the foot.

controlling the ball with and watch the ball onto the side of your foot (keep your eye on the ball at all times). As the ball meets your foot, immediately pull back or withdraw the inside of the foot. This will provide a cushioning effect and should leave the ball close to your foot but slightly ahead of you, so you can choose your next option with your second touch.

If you do not withdraw on impact, the ball is likely to bounce away from you and into the path of the opposition. The head should remain still throughout with eyes fixed on the ball.

Cushion control using the top of the foot
The technique
Once again it is important to be well balanced when you receive the ball. For this reason there are advantages to getting into line with the ball as early as possible so you are not stretching for the ball. Decide which foot you will be controlling the ball with and watch the ball onto the foot. For

Ball control using the top of the foot.

this technique you are likely to use your preferred kicking foot as this is a slightly more difficult technique than the inside of the foot. As the ball meets your foot, on the laces (the instep) of your boot, immediately withdraw or pull back your foot. You should see the ball cushioned and resting just in front of you. If the ball is a comfortable distance from your body then your second touch can be a pass, shot or dribble.

The head should remain still throughout the practice with eyes fixed on the ball.

Cushion control using the thigh
The technique
With all the ball control techniques it is important to be well balanced and composed as you receive the ball. The best chance of this happening is to get in line with the ball as quickly as possible. Depending on the flight of the ball and your positioning, you will need to select which thigh you are

Ball control using the thigh.

going to use to control the ball. After offering your thigh to the ball, as soon as contact is made, withdraw your leg. This should provide the cushioning effect for the ball to rest close to your feet, but just far enough away from you so your next touch can be a pass, dribble or shot. Keep your head still throughout with your eyes fixed on the ball. The ball will bounce away from you if you do not withdraw your thigh on impact with the ball.

Cushion control using the chest

The technique

This technique is very similar to the previous three techniques with the same principles applying. Be well balanced when receiving the ball. Get in line with the ball as quickly as possible and watch the ball onto the chest, with your head remaining steady. As the ball makes impact with the chest try to withdraw the surface by leaning back slightly. This will see the ball bounce up a little, but will provide the cushioning impact that will allow the ball to drop down near your feet to play your second touch.

Ball control using the chest.

In order to lean back, you will need to bend your knees. You will find that spreading your arms out slightly may well help with balance and can also help shielding the ball if marked by a defender.

> ## Top tip
>
> Cushion control is the most common way of bringing a ball under control. Whichever part of the body you use, the principle is the same: withdraw your controlling surface at the point of impact to stop the ball bouncing away.

Wedge control using the feet

The technique

A slightly more difficult technique to master than cushion control is wedge control when receiving a pass. With cushion control you withdraw or pull back the surface on impact with the ball. The wedge control is the opposite movement: immediately on impact you redirect the ball away from the body and into the available space. This technique of controlling the ball is more likely to be used if you do not have so much time to receive the ball.

As with the cushion control, it is important to be well balanced when you are receiving the ball, so you must move into the line of the ball as early as possible. Decide which foot you will be controlling the ball with and watch the ball onto your foot. You can use either the inside or outside of the foot for the first touch. As the ball meets your foot, immediately jab or push down so that the ball does not go too far away from you, but is played away into space.

Receiving and turning

It is a basic skill for any developing player to have the ability to turn with the ball as they receive it. Whenever a ball is played to you, one of the options for you is whether you can turn. Your body position is vital for this, so that you are looking to turn as you receive the ball.

Receiving the ball with an open body position

The earlier a young player is able to turn with the ball and look to receive the ball with an open body position, the quicker their game will develop. Receiving the ball this way allows play to be switched in a single movement. You only need to watch the top players to see how this is an automatic way for them to receive the ball. They are always checking behind them so that, if the opponent makes it difficult to turn, they can look to shield the ball or pass. If space and time permit, players should look to receive the ball with an open body position. This will allow them not only to switch play but also to see the whole pitch to help them decide what to do next.

The technique

As the ball is being passed to you, decide which foot you are going to receive it with. If you are receiving the ball with your right foot, then your left foot acts as an anchor. As the ball impacts onto your right foot and you cushion the impact of the ball, you should already be half turned to your right as you take the pace off the ball. The ball should carry on at a slower pace allowing you to complete your outward body turn quickly. The ball should still be under control while you face a new direction, ready to switch play or pass the ball down the channel. This technique is particularly useful for full-backs when they are receiving the ball from goalkeepers and need to look for passes into wide midfielders.

Top tip

The secret is to take most of the pace off the ball and turn at the same time to follow it – simple, but like all techniques it needs practising on the training ground.

Tackling

Dispossessing your opponent is the primary aim of tackling, and if you can emerge with the ball then you really have put your team in a strong position. However, if you have prevented your opponent from making progress then you have still done your job.

Statistic

Frank Lampard and Steven Gerrard will make a tackle, on average, every 19 minutes.

Tackling is a football fundamental. All players, no matter what position they play in, must have the technical ability to be able to tackle and defend for their team. As a midfielder you will be tackling in all areas of the pitch. Being able to close down the opposition and make tackles when needed can be of great value to your team. With players in possession seeming to have more and more protection from referees, it is extremely important that you time your tackle at the right time and in a fair manner. The chances of being booked or sent off are greater now than they have ever been. In this section we look at the techniques associated with:

- timing the tackle
- the block tackle
- the slide tackle.

Top tip

Be patient – only tackle if you are sure you can win the ball. After committing to the tackle, you could be left stranded with your opponent through on goal. Any player who charges into tackles without thinking is a liability to their team.

Principles of tackling

* A defender's first task is to delay the attacker by 'jockeying' – keeping your body between the attacker and the goal, backing off slightly as the attacker moves forward and waiting for the right moment to tackle. This delay tactic enables other players in your team the time to get back to defend. In preparation you should adopt the 'ready stance,' with knees bent, facing the opponent at an angle and watching the ball, not the movements of the player.

* You need to be fairly close to the player on the ball. If the time is right to make the tackle, this will allow you to get all your strength and weight behind the ball in an attempt to win it. Your ankle and knee should be locked solidly, which will maintain strength and at the same time reduce injury.

* You must try to get your foot behind the back of the ball when making the challenge. This way you will get more force behind the ball and reduce the chance of injuring your opponent with an 'over the top' tackle, which could see a player being seriously injured.

Jockeying an opponent

Timing the tackle

Timing a tackle is an art in itself. As a defender you must assess your options as quickly as possible to help you gain an advantage.

The technique

If your opponent does not have the ball under control and has their head down, then this may be your signal to make the tackle. If they have the ball under control and they are looking up weighing up their options, then it may be best to be cautious and patient and wait for the right time to tackle.

It is good practice to wait until your opponent pushes the ball out of their feet before making your challenge. When this happens the ball is furthest away from their body and not under direct control. When you feel the time is right to make the tackle, try to stay on your feet and not go to ground.

The block tackle

This is a very common tackle in the modern game. It is important to practise good technique.

The technique

You need to be reasonably close to the player in possession. When the time is right to make the tackle, the non-kicking foot is placed alongside the ball and the ankle joint and the knee of the tackling leg must be firm and locked. Your knees should be slightly bent, which lowers the centre of gravity and makes a more powerful and compact body shape. The ideal position for your head and upper body is over the ball. Some players may choose to make a fist with their hands, which tightens their upper body. The actual tackle is made with the kicking foot making contact through the middle and back of the ball. Although every player can practise the technique of tackling, success often comes down to a positive and aggressive attitude.

Block tackling an opponent.

The slide tackle

It is wise to use the slide tackle as a last resort because it involves you going to ground and takes you out of the game for a short time. After making the slide tackle, you should try to get back on your feet as quickly as possible. A slide tackle is one of the more difficult defensive skills to learn, though when done effectively and for good purpose it can add defensive qualities to you and your team.

The technique

With this particular tackle you approach the player with the ball from a side-on position. Keep your eye on the ball rather than on your opponent. As you turn sideways into the tackle, the arm nearest the opponent should be extended and reach for the ground to take your upper body weight as you slide to the ground. The leg closest to the ball and player should be allowed to collapse to enable you to get to the

Slide tackling on opponent.

ground quickly. While on the ground, your other leg should be extended to use a sweeping action to win the ball.

If you are unable to keep possession of the ball, then you should try to redirect the ball away from the player. After performing this tackle you must try to get back on your feet as quickly as possible, using your inside arm to lever yourself up.

Shooting

Statistic
A team that has **ten shots** on target is likely to win a match.

There is a saying in football – 'Never pass when you can shoot.' However, knowing when to shoot requires a split-second decision. Coaches will often encourage you to shoot if you get a chance or even a half chance. This relies on the player having the confidence and a positive attitude towards shooting at goal.

Shooting is the most important aspect of attacking play and therefore the requirement on players to practise their shooting technique is fundamental to them becoming a better player.

Top tip

You will miss more than you score when taking shots on goal, but you must remain positive about taking shots whenever the opportunity arises. However, remember to pass to a team-mate if they are in a better position to score.

Although there are many different techniques associated with shooting, the next section looks at two of the most common types:

- Shooting with the inside of the foot.
- The low driven shot.

Principles of shooting

- It is better to shoot wide than high because a shot going wide may still have some chance of being deflected into the goal.
- Accuracy is more important than power as a powerful shot off target merely presents the opposition with a goal kick.
- A low shot has more potential of beating the goalkeeper than a high shot, which goalkeepers find easier to save.
- Shots going away from a goalkeeper towards the far post are usually more difficult to save than shots to the near post. They also have more chance of coming into the path of another striker if the goalkeeper is unable to hold onto the shot.

Shooting with the inside of the foot

This particular shooting technique supports the idea that it is more important to be accurate than powerful, though both are ideal. Many players who shoot with the inside of the foot are at relatively close range of the goal because it is considered to be the most accurate technique. They are often 'picking their spot' and placing the ball past the keeper towards one corner of the net.

Shooting with the inside of the foot.

The technique

This is very similar technique to the push pass (see p. 93) though with a little more power. You should approach the ball from a slight angle and place your kicking foot alongside the ball. Your head remains steady and your eyes should be fixed on the ball. If you have time, take a quick look up and then back at the ball just before shooting to assess the position of the goalkeeper and the goal. Your shooting leg is taken back and contact is made with the ball through the inside of the foot coming into contact with the mid-line of the ball. The follow through is in the direction of the goal.

The low driven shot

Players who decide to shoot with the low driven shot technique are usually intent on gaining power as well as accuracy. They are also likely to have a positive mental attitude towards shooting. It is a common technique used when there is an opportunity to shoot from outside the penalty area, with power needed to beat the goalkeeper.

The technique

This particular technique is almost identical to the low driven pass technique (see p. 94), but obviously with more power. The approach is from a slight angle, with the non-kicking foot alongside and slightly in front of the ball. Your kicking foot should be fully extended as it makes contact with the back of the ball, which is struck with the laces (the instep) of the boot. The follow through takes place through the centre of the ball and in line with the intended target.

Shooting using low driven shot.

Quote | 'You mustn't be afraid to miss.'
(Mark Hughes)

Running with the ball

The technical ability to run confidently with the ball at their feet can make the difference between a good player and an average one. Practising this technique, once again, provides a player with a fundamental skill for playing the game.

A combination of strength and speed are required if you want to take the ball forward at your feet, beat defenders and get into the opposition's defensive third. It is a skill that benefits all players in a team. There is no better sight in the game than an accomplished defender or midfielder breaking forward with the ball to be part of an attack, or a striker turning with the ball and running at a defender.

The technique

You should aim to keep the ball approximately 1–2 m in front of you and use your arms to assist you with your running style and balance. Use the outside of your foot, or your instep (laces) to push the ball in front of you. Keep you head up so that you can see what is going on around you. Every few strides you may need to glance down to see the position of the ball. Try to increase your speed, using good arm and leg action while still keeping control of the ball.

Top tip

Don't let a player chasing you affect your concentration. If you get a chance, try to run across and in front of them. This may see them committing a foul on you as they try to track back.

Summary

- Midfielders need to be confident passers of the ball, using a variety of techniques to keep the ball in possession.

- When receiving the ball, be ready to turn and use cushion or wedge control techniques to keep the ball.

- Tackling is a basic skill for all players, with midfielders needing defensive qualities in all areas of the pitch.

- Shooting is a fundamental skill for attacking football, with practice needed to master the techniques.

- All players need to be confident with the ball at their feet, running in space or in front of opposition players.

Self testers

1 Describe the technique used for a push pass.

2 Is your body position leaning forward or back for a lofted pass?

3 What is the purpose of an open body position when receiving a pass?

4 Describe the basic technique of a block tackle.

Action plan

Practise these fundamental skills each week so that you increase your confidence in each of these aspects of play.

Chapter 8

Individual practice drills for midfielders

> THIS CHAPTER WILL:
> - Help you to develop the skills and techniques required to become an effective midfielder.
> - Provide drills and practices you can work on, either on your own or with a team-mate.

Chapter 7 highlighted the basic skills that all footballers need of passing, ball control when receiving the ball, tackling, shooting and running with the ball. Although these skills and techniques are fundamental for the developing player, there are also some specific individual skills and techniques required for the position of midfielder. Almost all of the technical skills for this position can be improved with practice. Look back at p. 27 in Chapter 1 to remind yourself of the key attributes of a good midfielder.

This chapter provides some examples of drills and practices that you can try on your own or with another team-mate to improve the fundamental skills and the more specific skills and techniques for the midfielder. The majority of the practices need another person to work with, although if you are on your own some of the practices can be adapted by using a rebound wall. If you are using a wall, please make sure it has a smooth finish, and that it is a safe area, not near to a road or windows.

Passing

Good players and good teams can keep possession of the ball because they have a wide range of passing techniques and the ability to know where to pass, what type of pass to use and when to pass. As mentioned in Chapter 7, there are many different types of pass that can be made in the modern game. Different parts of the foot and the body can be used to provide both short and long passes. The high level of ability often see when watching top players is only achieved as a result of many hours on the training pitch practising existing and new techniques.

This section highlights the techniques and suitable drills to help you develop the following range of passes:

- push pass
- lofted pass
- swerved pass.
- low driven pass
- chipped pass

Quote | How would you develop a good midfield player?
'From a young age I would encourage them to practise manipulating the ball so they can move the ball quickly and let it run across their body to play off either foot. I would try and develop their attitude to want the ball, to become competitive, be prepared to run beyond people and generally develop their mental strength.'
(Adrian Boothroyd)

The push pass

This is the most commonly used pass in the game and the one that is likely to be most accurate. This is mainly because the pass is made with the largest surface of the foot. A very popular pass when used over short distances.

DRILL 1: HIT THE TARGET

Purpose

To improve your technique for using a push pass, emphasizing pace and accuracy.

You need

4 cones

4 footballs

2 players

Activity

1   Use the cones to make a target area, a square 3 m × 3 m.

2   Players take turns to pass into the target area, approximately 15 m away.

3   Each player has two balls and uses the push pass technique.

4   A point is awarded for each ball finishing within the target area.

Think about

- Approaching the ball at a slight angle.

- Placing your non-kicking foot alongside the ball.

- Keeping your kicking foot turned outwards, showing the inside of the foot.

- Keeping your body over the ball and your eyes focussed on the ball.

Figure 8.1 **Drill 1: Hit the Target**

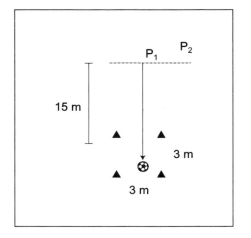
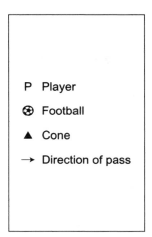

- Making sure the ankle of the kicking foot remains firm.
- Striking the middle of the ball with the inside of the foot.
- Making sure the kicking foot follows through towards the target area.

Target

- How many attempts do you need to score ten points?

Progression

- Reduce the target to a smaller area.
- Try the practice using your weaker foot.
- Try the practice with your team-mate serving a rolling ball to you. Redirect it using 'one touch' towards the target area.

DRILL 2: PASS WITH SPEED!

Purpose

To develop your ability to pass the ball at speed using the push pass technique.

You need

4 cones

1 football

2 players

Activity

1   Players stand opposite each other, 5 m apart just behind the line of cones.

2   Pass the ball to each other using the push pass.

3   Ball must be kept on the ground and struck firmly to cross the cone line.

4   Carry out the practice for 60 seconds and see how many passes you can make.

5   A point is scored for each pass that crosses the line on the ground.

Think about

- Using the correct technique as described in 'Hit the target' (p. 120).
- Not allowing the focus on speed see you lose the quality of the pass.
- Remaining on your toes so you can react quickly.
- Making passes firm and accurate.
- Keeping your body and head over the ball.

Figure 8.2 **Drill 2: Pass with speed!**

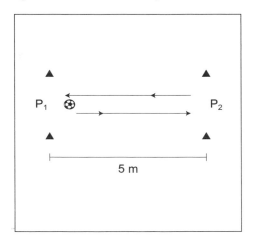
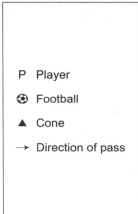

Target

- Can you make 30 passes in a minute?

Progression

- Increase the distance between the cones to 10 m apart.
- Restrict the practice to one touch–first time passing – and only count the passes which are completed this way.
- Try the practice using your weaker foot.

The low driven pass

This type of pass is most useful if a player wants to pass the ball over a longer distance and wants the ball to arrive quickly. The ball stays low to the ground so obviously there needs to be a clear route between the passer and the receiver.

DRILL 3: KNOCK THEM OVER

Purpose

To improve your technique for using the low driven pass, with an emphasis on accuracy.

You need

8 cones/boxes/targets

1 football

2 players

Activity

1 Two players stand approximately 15 m apart, one player with the ball.

2 Targets (cones/boxes) are placed down in a line halfway between the two players.

3 Targets can be grouped together or left as single targets (harder).

4 Try to knock down each target using the low driven pass technique.

5 Take alternative passes at the targets.

Think about

- Approaching the ball at a slight angle.
- Keeping your body position over the ball – eyes on the ball.
- Placing your non-kicking foot alongside the ball, though slightly in front.

Figure 8.3 **Drill 3: Knock them over**

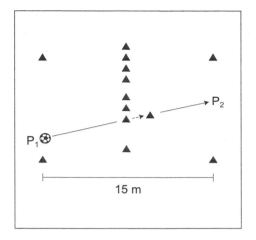
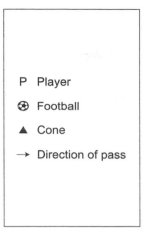

- Keeping your kicking foot extended, making the pass with the top of your foot.

- Following through with your kicking foot, in the line of the intended target.

- The accuracy of your pass, not just the power.

Target

- Can you knock down all eight targets in less than 30 passes?

Progression

- Spread out the targets so they are not grouped together.

- Increase the grid size to 25 m so you are further away from the targets.

The lofted pass

The lofted pass is most appropriate when players are looking to play a long pass over the head of a player or several players, often used when switching play or counter-attacking. Many of the top players are able to play extremely accurate passes over long distances into the paths of their team-mates.

DRILL 4: LONG BUT ACCURATE

Purpose

To practise the mechanics and technique of the lofted pass with emphasis on accuracy.

You need

4 cones

6 footballs

2 players

Activity

1   Use cones to make a target zone measuring 10 m × 10 m.

2   You need to stand 30 m away and play a lofted pass into the target zone.

3   Player 2 stands behind the target zone and checks that the pass bounces into the zone, acting as a referee.

4   Win a point for every successful long lofted pass. Points are not scored if the ball bounces before reaching the target zone.

Think about

• Approaching the ball at an angle.

• Keeping your head still and eyes on the ball.

• Taking a larger last stride into the ball to assist with the swinging motion of your kicking leg.

Figure 8.4 **Drill 4: Long but accurate**

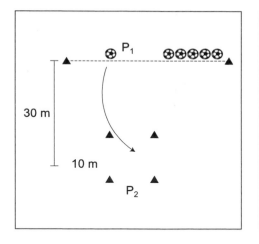

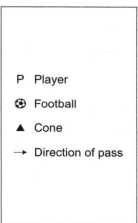

P　Player

⊕　Football

▲　Cone

→　Direction of pass

- Placing your non-kicking foot alongside the ball, though slightly behind.
- Making contact with the back of the ball with your instep (top of the foot).
- Remembering to follow through your kicking foot in the line of target.

Target

- Keep your score after ten passes and then try to beat your score with a further ten passes.

Progression

- Increase the distance to the target zone.
- Reduce the size of the target zone to 5 m × 5 m.

The chipped pass

If players can master the chip pass it has a real advantage over some other passes. The chip pass allows you to play the ball over the opposition's head within a relatively short distance. This pass is extremely difficult to intercept and is ideal for attackers to receive in the last third of the pitch and to run on beyond the last line of defence.

DRILL 5: CHIP AWAY

Purpose

To practise your technique and accuracy of chipping the ball.

You need

4 cones

1 football

2 players

Activity

1 Stand opposite a team-mate in a grid 15 m apart.

2 With a ball at your feet try to chip the ball into the hands of the other player.

3 Player 2 moves along the line between the two cones to present a different target.

4 Score two points each time the ball is caught by the other player.

Think about

- Approaching the ball at a slight angle.
- Planting your non-kicking foot alongside but slightly in front of the ball.
- Having your head and upper body slightly over the ball.

Figure 8.5 **Drill 5: Chip away**

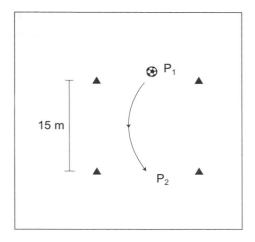

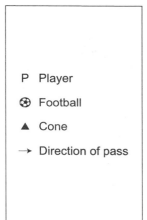

P   Player

⊕   Football

▲   Cone

→   Direction of pass

- The kicking leg being withdrawn more from the knee than the hip.

- The kicking foot making contact with the underside of the ball, via a stabbing action.

- Increasing the backspin on the ball by applying a more powerful stabbing action.

Target

- Can you make five consecutive successful chips?

- Set yourself a new target increasing your best score.

Progression

- Your team-mate rolls the ball underarm to you so that the chip pass is made from a moving ball rather than a stationary one.

- Extend the distance to 20 m.

- Try the practice using your weaker foot.

The swerved pass

The swerved pass is another pass that is used over longer distances with, as its name suggests, a swerve in its flight. This technique is applied when a player wants to swerve the ball around a player or a wall, as the swerved pass is technically the same as a swerved shot.

DRILL 6: CURVE AND SWERVE

Purpose

To practise the required technique to produce a swerved pass.

You need

6 cones

1 football

2 players

Activity

1   Two players stand 15 m apart within a grid marked by four cones. Place the remaining two cones in the centre of the grid.

2   Player 1 with the ball plays a swerved pass around the two cones in the centre of the grid.

3   Player 2 receives the ball, controls it and repeats the practice.

4   Each player scores a point for a successful swerved pass.

5   To score a point the receiving player must not have to move more than 1 m from their starting position.

Think about

- Approaching the ball at a slight angle, focusing on the ball.

- Making contact with the side of the ball rather than directly behind it.

- Placing your non-kicking foot alongside the ball.

- Contact with the kicking foot is made with the inside or outside of the foot depending which way you are swerving the pass.

Figure 8.6 **Drill 6: Curve and swerve**

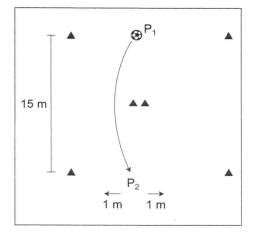
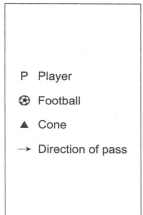

Target

- Try to make five consecutive point scoring passes.

Progression

- Widen the two cones in the centre of the grid, requiring more swerve on the pass.
- Increase the distance between the two players to 20 m.
- Try the swerve pass with the outside of the foot.

Ball control

The first touch a player has on the ball is crucial as it can mean the difference between keeping possession and losing it. If you work on these practices then your technique should improve and you can move to the next stage of deciding what to do with the ball, rather than worrying about your control technique.

The following drills provide you with technique and skills practice to develop your:

- **cushion control**
- **wedge control.**

Cushion control

With this method of control, a player withdraws or pulls back the surface controlling the ball on impact. This cushions the ball so it falls to the ground in a position where a player can then make their pass, shot or dribble with their next touch. The controlling surface could be the head, chest, thigh or feet.

DRILL 7: CUSHION IT!

Purpose

To practise and improve your ability to control the ball using cushion control.

You need

4 cones   1 football   2 players

Activity

1   Work with another player inside a 10 m × 10 m grid.

2   Player 2 (the server) has the ball and throws the ball underarm yet above head height to you so that you can control it with your thigh.

3   Use cushion control to bring the ball down and pass the ball back to the server.

4   Continue this, moving around the grid.

5   One point is awarded for each successful control.

Think about

•   Getting into the line of the flight of the ball.

•   Selecting the controlling surface – your thigh.

•   Keeping your eye on the ball as it approaches.

•   Being relaxed.

•   Withdrawing the thigh as the ball makes contact to absorb the pace and cushion the ball.

•   Making an accurate push pass back to the server.

Figure 8.7 **Drill 7: Cushion it!**

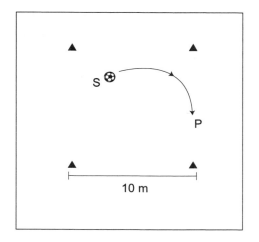

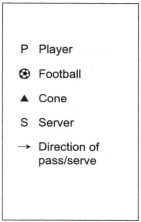

P   Player

⊛   Football

▲   Cone

S   Server

→   Direction of
     pass/serve

Target

* Ten successful control and pass manoeuvres – consecutively.

Progression

* Increase the distance between the two players.
* Server moves around the grid so that you need to look up after controlling the ball to find the server.
* Control using both left and right feet.
* Consider the same activity with different forms of serving so that different parts of the body are used to practise the cushion control (for example, chest, inside foot).

Wedge control

Another method of controlling the ball, when time and space is available, is the wedge control. A player pushes out the surface chosen (head, chest, thigh or feet) to control the ball, so that the ball is redirected into the space for the player's second touch.

DRILL 8: WEDGE WORKS

Purpose

To develop your ability to bring the ball under control using the wedge technique.

You need

4 cones

1 football

2 players

Activity

1 Stand approximately 20 m away from another player (Player 2).

2 Move towards Player 2 and receive a pass to your feet.

3 Use wedge control, redirecting the ball out of your feet with your first touch.

4 With your second touch pass back to Player 2 who controls the ball before passing it back to you.

5 Keep moving back to your line to receive the pass.

6 Score one point for each successful control.

Think about

• Getting into the line of the flight of the ball.

• Selecting your controlling surface – inside of foot.

• Keeping your eye on the ball as it approaches.

Figure 8.8 **Drill 8: Wedge works**

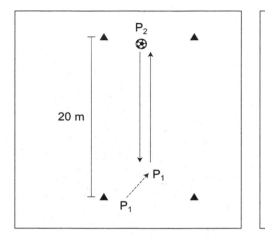

- Tensing the controlling surface – the foot – as you receive the ball.
- Redirecting the ball out in front of you.

Target

- Be confident receiving the ball on your weaker side.
- Keep a score out of ten passes. Can you beat that score for another set of ten passes?

Progression

- Increase the speed of the practice.
- Use your right and left foot alternatively.
- Increase the size of the grid and move freely around the area – varying the serve to the thigh, chest and feet.

Heading

People will often comment that football is at its best when the ball is played on the ground. However, there are inevitably going to be situations in a game when the ball is played in the air through goal kicks, free kicks, corners, long throws, crosses and clearances.

Heading the ball is generally divided into two categories – defensive heading and attacking heading – though there are some common principles that apply to both. If the correct technique is followed, then heading a football will not hurt and, with regular practice, a player's confidence will grow.

Whether you are making a defensive or attacking header it is important that you follow the basic technique:

- **Be prepared to attack the ball.**
- **The movement of the neck muscles provides the power supported by some upper body movement/arched back.**
- **The ball should come into contact with the forehead because this is the largest and flattest part of the head surface, enabling the player to control their heading and provide accuracy.**
- **After contact is made with the ball, there should be a follow through of the head along the line of the intended target.**

Basic heading

DRILL 9: BASIC HEADERS

Purpose

To develop confidence and practise the basic heading technique.

You need

4 cones　1 football　2 players

Activity

1　**Players stand opposite each other within a 5 m × 5 m grid.**

2 Player 1 throws the ball underarm to Player 2 who heads the ball back.

3 Players alternate roles with Player 2 throwing the ball to Player 1.

4 Players score a point for every successful header.

Figure 8.9 **Drill 9: Basic headers**

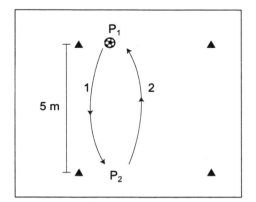
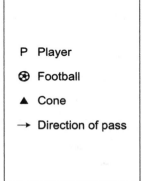

Think about

- Watching the ball.
- Moving into the line of the ball.
- Keeping your eyes open.
- Heading the ball with the forehead.
- Aiming to make contact with the middle of the ball.
- Attacking the ball with purpose.

Target

- Ten consecutive, accurate headers to your partner.

Progression

- Increase the distance between the two players to 10 m.

The following practices will encourage you to develop confidence and good technique with heading the football, whether you are in a defensive or attacking situation. The types of headers are as follows:

- defensive headers
- flick on headers
- attacking headers
- diving headers.

Defensive headers

As a defending player, particularly when the ball is close to your team's penalty area, it is important to:

- Head the ball high, which allows for time for defending team-mates to reorganize.
- Head the ball long, which takes the ball further away from the danger area.
- Head the ball wide, either out of play or to a safe angle from the goal.

DRILL 10: HEADING FOR SAFETY

Purpose

To improve the technique involved when heading for distance.

You need

4 cones

1 football

3 players

Activity

1 Player 1 stands 20 m away from player 3. Player 2 stands in between them.
2 Player 2 serves the ball for Player 1 to head.
3 Player 1 tries to head the ball beyond the server to Player 3.
4 Player 3 collects the ball and returns it to Player 2 to continue the practice.

Figure 8.10 **Drill 10: Heading for safety**

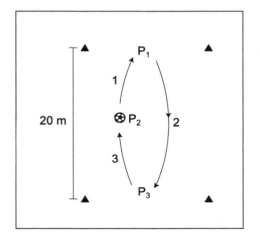
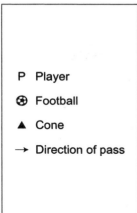

5 Rotate positions every ten headers.
6 Players score a point for clearing the middle player and two points for reaching Player 3.

Think about

• Heading the ball high.
• Heading the ball long.
• Attacking the ball with confidence.
• Running to meet the ball.
• Slightly arching your back and tightening your neck muscles.
• Accurate serving.

Target

• First player to reach ten points after an equal number of turns.

Progression

• Continue using three players, but slightly reorganize the roles:
  • Player 2 stands just in front of Player 1 but remains static.
  • Player 3 becomes the server. As Player 3 serves the ball to Player 1, Player 1 jumps to head clear.

- Players rotate roles.
- The role of Player 2 can change so they can offer more resistance by also jumping to distract Player 1.

Flick on headers

The flick on header is used in a variety of different situations. Players may use the technique in an attacking situation to head towards goal from either a corner or long throw. Alternatively, a forward may use the flick on header to put a team-mate through on goal, flicking the ball beyond the last defender. In defensive situations, a player may use the flick on header to head the ball backwards to their goalkeeper as a safe way of keeping possession.

DRILL 11: FLICK IT ON

Purpose

To improve the technique involved in flick on headers.

You need

4 cones

1 football

3 players

Activity

1 Player 1 serves the ball underarm to Player 2 who stands in the middle of a 10 m × 10 m grid marked by cones.

2 Player 2 heads the ball to Player 3 with a flick on header.

3 Player 3 collects the ball and serves it to Player 2.

4 Players rotate their positions after ten headers.

5 One point is scored for accurate flick on headers reaching the intended targets.

Think about

- Moving quickly into the flight of the ball.

Figure 8.11 **Drill 11: Flick it on**

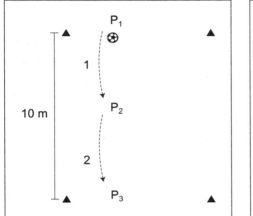
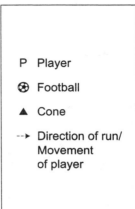

- Using one foot to take off as you jump.
- Trying to head the ball at its highest point.
- Using your forehead to deflect the ball.
- Tilting your head back so the ball glances off your forehead towards the intended target.

Target

- First player to reach ten points after an equal number of turns.

Progression

- Introduce a defender by moving Player 3 to stand behind Player 2. Player 2 then tries to flick the ball on and over Player 3 making it a more realistic game situation.

Statistic
Over 20% of all goals scored are from headers.

Attacking headers

When teams are attacking in the last third of the pitch, they will often find that space on the ground is harder to find. As a deliberate tactic they will look to put the ball in the air, particularly in and around the penalty area. Players who head the ball in attacking situations are usually looking to head for accuracy, either on goal or into the path of another player on their team. Headers on goal that are aimed downwards are generally the most difficult to save.

DRILL 12: HEADING AT A TARGET

Purpose

To develop heading technique with emphasis on accuracy.

You need

10 cones or boxes

1 football

2 players

Activity

1   Players face each other 10 m apart.

2   Player 1 throws the ball up for headers at a target area (cones) in the centre of the grid.

3   Player 2 collects the ball and repeats the practice.

4   Two points are scored for every successful header. The ball must not bounce before reaching the target area.

5   Develop the practice with players serving to each other and heading towards the target.

Think about

• Establishing a well-balanced stance.

• Releasing the ball out of your hands.

• Attacking the ball with your forehead and with your eyes open.

Figure 8.12 **Drill 12: Heading at a target**

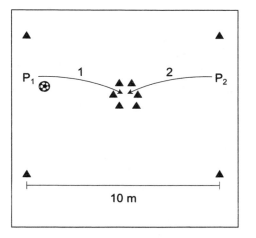
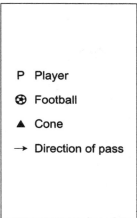

- Developing the power by swinging your upper body backwards and then forwards.

- Developing your jump so that you get your timing right.

Target

- First player to score ten points.

Progression

- Use four cones to mark out two 3 m wide goals 10 m apart:

  - Players cannot use their hands when defending their goal.

  - Player 1 serves the ball from the goal line to Player 2 who heads the ball down and past Player 1, towards the corner of the goal.

  - Two points for every goal scored, one point for every saved header on target.

  - Aim – first player to get ten points after an equal number of turns.

Diving headers

All heading is about attacking the ball and possibly the best example of this is the diving header, where the whole body is committed to the ball. The diving header is often seen as an attacking skill, though it can be used in defensive situations to prevent goals being scored.

DRILL 13: DIVING PAYS

Purpose

To develop the technique and confidence to produce a diving header.

You need

4 cones

1 football

2 players

Activity

1   Players face each other 10 m apart.

2   Player 1 throws the ball to Player 2; the ball should drop just in front of Player 2.

3   Player 2 attempts to score past Player 1 with a diving header.

4   Two points for every goal scored, one point for every header on target.

Think about

• Making the serves accurate.

• Keeping your eye on the ball.

• Trying to head the top of the ball, forcing it downwards.

• Heading the ball with your forehead with eyes open.

• Dropping your arms to cushion your fall.

• Aiming for the corner of the goal.

• Attacking the header in a committed way.

Figure 8.13 **Drill 13: Diving pays**

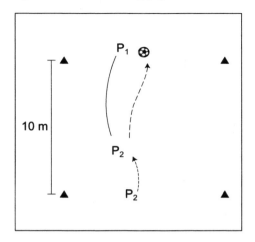

Target

• Reaching ten points after ten attempts.

Progression

• Introduce two more players, widen the goals and play 2 v 2 – taking it in turns to serve to each other in your teams to score diving headers.

Shooting

The techniques for shooting are simply an extension of good passing techniques, which have been covered in both this chapter and Chapter 7. This is why shooting is often described as 'passing' the ball past the goalkeeper and into the net.

Players should possess a wide range of shooting techniques regardless of the position they play in. A variety of techniques for shooting are used depending on the situation. There are, however, some principles that never change:

- **The head should be kept down and steady.**
- **Concentrate on accuracy, making sure you hit the target.**
- **Strike through the ball.**
- **Observe the position of the defenders and goalkeeper.**
- **Pick your target – the area of the goal which you feel gives you the most chance of scoring.**

These practices help to develop your technique for the following shots:

- **The first-time shot.**
- **The low driven shot.**
- **The instep volley.**
- **The half volley.**
- **Shooting on the run.**
- **The curling shot.**
- **The lob.**

Statistic

60% of all goals scored are from within 10 m of the goal and almost 75% of these goals are as a result of a first-time strike.

The first-time shot

DRILL 14: SHOOT FIRST TIME

Purpose

To encourage you to shoot first time.

You need

4 cones

4 footballs

3 players

Activity

1 The server and Player 1 stand 20 m away from the goalkeeper.

2 The server feeds a short pass to you, aiming in front of you so that you can run on to the ball.

2 Sprint after the pass and shoot first time at the goal.

3 Score two points for each goal and one point for every shot on target.

Figure 8.14 **Drill 14: Shoot first time**

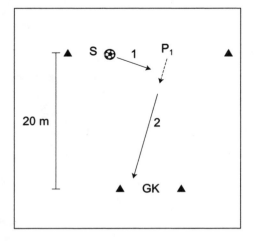

P	Player
⊕	Football
▲	Cone
GK	Goalkeeper
S	Server
→	Direction of pass
--→	Direction of run/ Movement of player

Think about

*   Reacting quickly to the pass.

*   Keeping your eye on the ball.

*   Trying to shoot with either foot.

*   Approaching the ball at the correct angle, to get your shot away.

*   Approaching the shot with a positive attitude.

Target

*   Hit the target with every shot – accuracy is more important than power.

*   Try to score more than ten points from ten shots.

Progression

*   The server can follow their pass and put pressure on you, acting as a defender.

*   Vary the type of serve, so you need to consider applying different techniques such as volley, half-volley or swerved shot.

The low driven shot

DRILL 15: KEEP IT LOW AND HIT THE CORNERS

Purpose

To improve your technical ability to shoot, using the driven shot.

You need

6 cones

1 football

3 players

Activity

1   Three players are positioned in a grid measuring 30 m × 30 m.

2   A goalkeeper is in the middle of the grid, protecting the goal.

3   The other two players are at each end of the grid and take it in turns to shoot at the goal.

4   If the goalkeeper saves the shot they turn and roll the ball back to the other player.

5   Players must remain on their toes to help retrieve the ball if the ball goes past the goalkeeper.

6   Two points are scored for every goal.

7   Players alternate roles.

Think about

*   Keeping the ball below shoulder height.

*   Approaching the ball at a slight angle.

*   Getting your non-kicking foot alongside, and slightly in front of, the ball.

*   Aiming for the corners of the goal.

*   Keeping your kicking foot extended so the top of your foot strikes the back of the ball.

*   Getting your kicking foot to follow through in line with the corner of the goal.

Figure 8.15 **Drill 15: Keep it low and hit the corners**

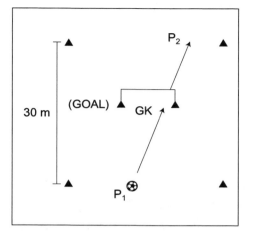
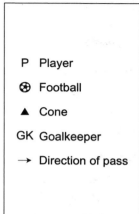

Target

- First player to reach ten points.

Progression

- Make the practice two touch – use the first touch to receive the ball and set it up, the second touch should be the low driven shot – on either the right or left foot.

The instep volley

DRILL 16: ON THE VOLLEY

Purpose

To develop your technical ability to use the instep volley.

You need

3 cones

1 football

3 players

Activity

1   Three players take part in this practice, one being the server, and stand 5 m apart from each other.

2   The server throws the ball to Player 1 who volleys the ball back.

3   The server then turns slightly to repeat the practice with Player 2.

4   Player 1 and Player 2 have ten volleys each and then players rotate their roles.

5   A point is scored for every volley returned to the server without bouncing.

Think about

- Using your arms to keep your balance.
- Extending your foot by pointing your toes, which will help to keep the ball down.
- The ball making contact with the instep – the top of the foot.
- Keeping your head still.
- Following through the kicking leg which will maintain the control, speed and direction of the volley.
- Striking the ball cleanly.

Figure 8.16 **Drill 16: On the volley**

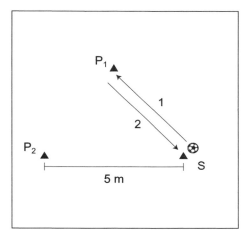

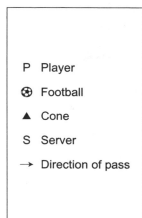

P   Player

⊕   Football

▲   Cone

S   Server

→   Direction of pass

Target

- Practise equally with both feet.
- First player to reach 20 points after equal turns.

Progression

- The same number of players can progress the activity with a practice to improve the technique of the side volley. At a similar distance apart, take it in turns to serve to one player who side volleys it to the third player.

- Change the action to a swivel and volley; as you receive the ball rotate your body so that you face the intended target. Use your arms to help your balance and keep watching the ball. Using the same part of the foot, you should try to strike over the ball to keep it down.

- The practice can be further developed by a player crossing the ball to you so that you can attempt a volley at goal.

The half-volley

DRILL 17: CONNECT ON THE BOUNCE

Purpose

To develop your technical ability to shoot using the half-volley.

You need

4 cones

1 football

2 players

Activity

1　Two players work together in a grid measuring 10 m × 10 m.

2　Player 1, with the ball, drops the ball in front of them and half-volleys it to Player 2.

3　Player 2 collects the ball and repeats the practice.

4　One point for every successful half-volley that ends up in the receiver's arms, without the ball bouncing.

Figure 8.17 **Drill 17: Connect on the bounce**

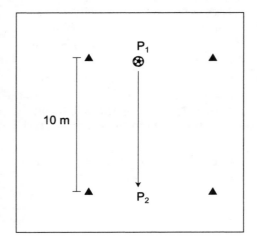
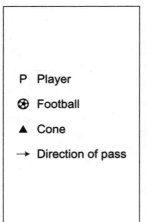

Think about

- Keeping your eyes on the ball as it drops in front of you.
- Using your arms to maintain balance.
- Getting your standing foot alongside the ball.
- Pointing your foot down and making contact with the ball just after it bounces.
- Hitting straight through the ball.
- Creating power by an accurate and controlled follow through.
- Concentrating on timing.

Target

- Try the practice using your right and left foot.
- First player to reach ten points.

Progression

- Increase the distance between the two players so that you can actually take shots at each other. Use the cones to represent a goal. First player to score ten goals using the half-volley.

Shooting on the run

DRILL 18: ON THE RUN

Purpose

To develop your decision making for shooting on the run.

You need

8 cones or markers

Several footballs

3 players

Activity

1   Server stands alongside Player 1, approximately 20 m from the goal. A goalkeeper defends the goal.

2   The server plays a ball forward towards a halfway line.

3   Player 1 moves quickly to chase the pass and assesses the options for a shot on goal.

4   Player 1 must shoot before the ball crosses the halfway line.

5   The server varies the type of pass.

6   One point is scored for every shot on target and two points for every goal.

7   Players rotate roles.

Think about

*   Assessing your options depending on the type of serve:

    –   Do you need to control the ball or can you shoot first time?

    –   A rolling ball will possibly mean a low driven shot is recommended.

    –   A bouncing ball may require you to volley or half-volley the ball.

*   Being confident, hitting through the ball and following through in the line of target.

Figure 8.18 **Drill 18: On the run**

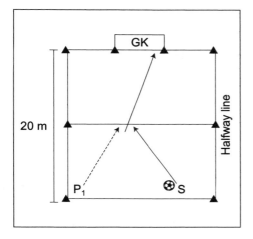
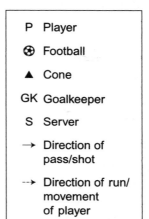

Target

- Hitting the target with every shot.
- Scoring with 50 per cent of the shots you take.

Progression

- A fourth player can be introduced acting as a defender.
- The server can follow their pass and apply pressure to you as the shooter.
- The server could change their position so some serves are coming from the side, some from behind and some in front of you.

The curling shot

DRILL 19: CURL IT IN

Purpose

To develop your ability to deliver an accurate curling shot.

You need

6 cones

Several footballs

3 players

Activity

1   Three players work together in a 15 m × 15 m grid. One player is the goalkeeper.

2   You need to stand approximately 15 m from the goal, ready to deliver a curling shot on goal.

3   The defender stands approximately 10 m away from you, in line with the right-hand post, and defends.

4   Curl the ball around the defender and into the corner of the goal.

5   One point for hitting the post, two points for shots on target and three points for a goal.

6   Players rotate roles.

Think about

•   Keeping your head down as you approach the ball.

•   Using your arms to maintain balance.

•   Placing your standing foot alongside the ball.

•   Creating a high back swing with your kicking leg.

•   Trying to curl your foot right around the ball to impart spin – using the inside of your foot.

•   Striking the ball hard to get more curve.

•   Remembering to follow through.

Figure 8.19 **Drill 19: Curl it in**

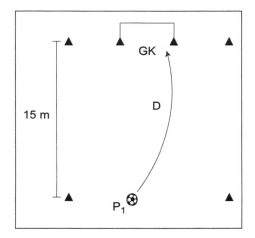 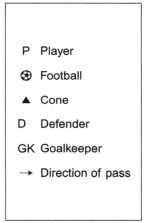

Target

* Take both right-footed and left-footed shots.

* Hit the target with at least six out of ten shots.

* How many shots are needed to reach 20 points?

Progression

* Move the defending player to create a more difficult target (requiring more curl).

* Try to curl a shot using the outside of your foot. The same activity can be used.

The lob

DRILL 20: OVER AND IN

Purpose

To develop your technical ability to lob the ball – particularly over an advancing goalkeeper.

You need

6 cones   1 football   2 players

Activity

1   Work with a goalkeeper in a 15 m × 15 m grid.

2   Drop the ball in front of you and after it has bounced try to lob the ball over the goalkeeper and into the goal.

3   At the same time as the ball is dropped, the goalkeeper should walk forward approximately 5 m.

4   Try to lob the ball over the head of the advancing goalkeeper but get the ball to drop into the goal.

5   Two points for every goal scored.

6   Players alternate positions.

Think about

• Keeping your eye on the ball as it bounces in front of you.

• Using your arms to help you balance.

• Adjusting your body position so that the ball is within reach.

• Striking through the ball with your instep (top of the foot) and rising up onto your toes on your standing foot.

• Varying the power of your strike and the length of your follow through; his will alter the ball's flight.

Target

• Try the lobbed shot with both your left and right foot.

• How many shots do you need to score 20 points?

Figure 8.20 **Drill 20: Over and in**

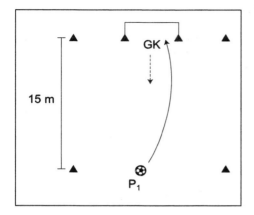 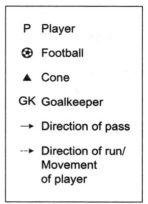

Progression

- Alter the distance so you get used to developing a lobbed shot from closer to and further away from goal.

- Introduce a third player, players practise lobbing the ball over each other's heads in a relay style: Player 1 drops the ball in front of them and lobs the ball over Player 2, who starts running towards Player 1 to take their place. Player 1 runs to the centre of the practice for Player 3, having just received the first pass, to lob the ball over player 1 and swap places. The practice continues in this way.

Figure 8.21 **Progression**

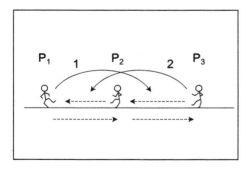

Dribbling

The ability to dribble the ball with confidence, demonstrating good technique, is required all over the pitch. In the attacking third of the pitch, players are encouraged to run at defenders and be as creative as possible as they try to break down the last line of the defence. In the middle third of the pitch, players will often dribble away from player's challenges as they look for space to pass or shoot. In the defensive third, defenders will often dribble when confronted with tight situations, though generally dribbling in this third of the pitch is kept to a minimum, to avoid being caught in possession.

Although dribbling can be one of the most entertaining football skills, players should generally only dribble when there is not a good passing option. The following two practices will build confidence and technique.

Individual dribbling practice

DRILL 21: THROUGH THE CONES

Purpose

To develop your ability to control and dribble the ball.

You need

12 cones or markers

2 footballs

2 players

Activity

1   Players have a ball each and dribble between a set of cones.

2   Both players initially dribble up their line of cones and then cross over at the top of the line.

3   Each player dribbles down the other line, then, when they reach the last cone, turn and dribble between the two cones marking the finish.

4   The first player to reach the finish cone is the winner.

Figure 8.22 **Drill 21: Through the cones**

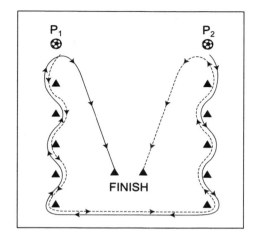

Think about

- Maintaining close control over the ball, with lots of touches.
- Building up your speed gradually.
- Using different surfaces of the foot to dribble: the inside, outside and sole (bottom) of the foot.
- Try to look beyond the ball at the cones you are approaching.

Target

- Play a 'best of five' match. If one player is a lot quicker than the other, start from different positions to even it up.
- Make sure you practise dribbling on the course using your weaker foot.

Progression

- Extend the course and move the cones closer together so that the necessary controlling skills are increased.

Dribbling practice in a 1 v 1 situation

DRILL 22: LEAVE THEM BEHIND

Purpose

To develop a player's ability to use dribbling moves to leave their opponent behind.

You need

2 cones   1 football   2 players

Activity

1   Two cones are placed 10 m apart.

2   Face another player, the defender, across the line of the two cones.

3   Players must stay their side of the cone line at all times.

4   With the ball at your feet, use body feints and dribbling moves to unbalance the defender.

5   To score a point you must reach one of the cones before the defender and stop the ball next to the cone.

6   The defender can stop a goal by getting to the cone first and putting their foot on it.

7   No tackling takes place.

Think about

•   Moving the ball across your body using both feet.

•   Dropping your shoulder, bending your knees and taking the ball away in the opposite direction.

•   Stopping and starting your dribble.

•   Stepping over the ball with one foot and then taking it in the other direction.

•   Using body feints to unbalance the defender.

•   Accelerating away.

Figure 8.23 **Drill 22: Leave them behind**

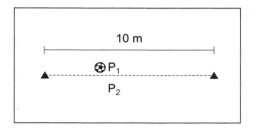

Target

How many goals can you score in three minutes?

Progression

- Attacking the corners
  - Player 2 passes the ball to Player 1 who dribbles the ball to either of the two corner cones.
  - Player 2 acts as the defender. Player 1 uses dribbling moves to unbalance the defender and dribble at a vacant cone.
  - The two cones provide targets to encourage the attacker to dribble past either side of the defender.

Figure 8.24 **Attacking the corners**

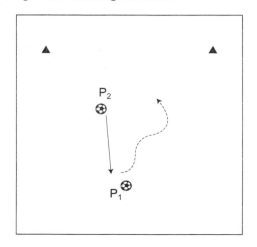
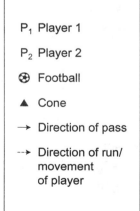

Turning

There are numerous turns that a player can practise and master, and you will often find that players will have their favourite ones. This is not a problem, although if you only have the skill to perform one turn, then you will become easy to defend against. Players need the ability to turn quickly and effectively for the following reasons:

- **To create space.**
- **To change the direction of play.**
- **To lose a marker.**

Whatever turns are being delivered, the two most important principles to remember are:

1 **Slow into the turn.**
2 **Accelerate away.**

Some of the most popular turns to practise are:

- The inside hook.
- The outside hook.
- The drag back.
- The Cruyff turn.

The inside hook

DRILL 23: TURNING WITH OPPOSITION – THE INSIDE HOOK

Purpose

To develop the ability to turn with the ball, using the inside hook.

You need

5 cones   2 footballs   2 players

Activity

1 Players each have a ball and face each other in a 10 m × 10 m grid.

2   Both players dribble the ball to the middle of the grid, marked by a cone.

3   As they reach the cone they turn away from each other using an inside hook turn and dribble back to their starting point.

4   They have a few seconds' rest and then repeat the exercise.

5   Players should work together so they arrive at the centre cone together.

Think about

- Making the defender (the cone) think you are going to strike the ball – by faking to shoot.

- Stopping the ball, then cutting it across you as you turn – do this by taking a long stride forward, then reach for and 'hook' the ball with the inside of the front foot.

- Pivoting on your back foot.

- Turning your body in the same direction as the ball has been 'hooked'.

- Keeping your body low.

- Turning away from the cone (the defender) and accelerating away.

Figure 8.25 **Drill 23: Turning with opposition – the inside hook**

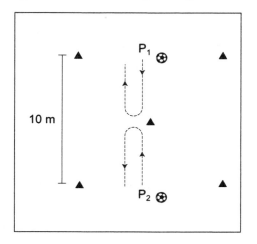
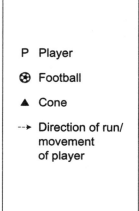

P   Player

⊕   Football

▲   Cone

--→   Direction of run/ movement of player

Target

- Do not sacrifice quality by doing the turn too quickly.
- Develop your acceleration out of the turn.
- Try the practice using your weaker foot.

Progression

- Use only one ball and six cones to create an attacker v defender situation.
    - Player 1 has possession of the ball within the grid and Player 2 acts as a defender.
    - Player 1 dribbles the ball into the centre of the grid and attempts to lose the defender by using a turn to create a space. Use a variety of different turns, be creative and accelerate away.
    - Player 1 can score by dribbling through one of the small target goals.

Figure 8.26 **Progression**

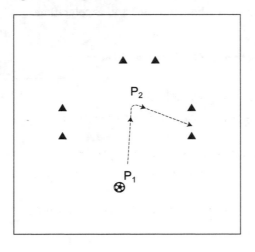
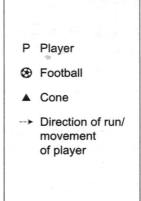

P   Player

⊕   Football

▲   Cone

--→   Direction of run/ movement of player

The outside hook

Purpose

To develop your ability to turn with the ball, using the outside hook.

You need

5 cones

2 footballs

2 players

Activity

1   Players each have a ball and face each other in a 10 m × 10 m grid.

2   Both players dribble the ball to the middle of the grid, marked by a cone.

3   As they reach the cone, they turn away from each other using an outside hook turn and dribble back to their starting point.

4   They have a few seconds' rest and then repeat the exercise.

5   Players should work together so they arrive at the centre cone together.

Think about

•   Planting your standing foot alongside the ball.

•   Swinging your playing foot at the ball, lifting it over and past the ball.

•   Dropping your right shoulder if you are turning to the right.

•   Hooking the ball behind you with the outside of your playing foot.

•   Turning your body 180° so you can follow in the line of the ball.

Figure 8.27 **Drill 24: Turning with opposition – the outside hook**

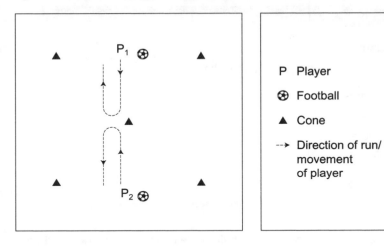

Target

- Try the practice using your weaker foot.
- Develop the speed gradually, concentrating on quality and technique.

Progression

- Use only one ball and six cones to create an attacker v defender situation.
  - Player 1 has possession of the ball within the grid and Player 2 acts as a defender.

- Player 1 dribbles the ball into the centre of the grid and attempts to lose the defender by using a turn to create a space. Use a variety of different turns, be creative and accelerate away.

- Player 1 can score by dribbling through one of the small target goals.

Figure 8.28 **Progression**

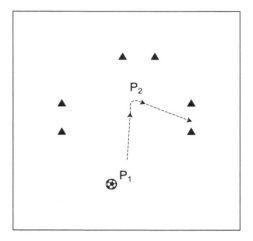

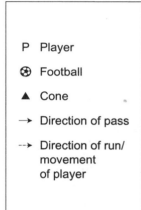

P   Player

⊕   Football

▲   Cone

→   Direction of pass

⇢   Direction of run/ movement of player

The drag back

DRILL 25: TURNING WITH OPPOSITION – THE DRAG BACK

Purpose

To develop your ability to turn the ball using the drag back.

You need

5 cones

2 footballs

2 players

Activity

1   Players each have a ball and face each other in a 10 m × 10 m grid.

2   Both players dribble the ball to the middle of the grid, marked by a cone.

3   As they reach the cone, they turn away from each other using a drag back, and dribble back to their starting point.

4   They have a few seconds' rest and then repeat the exercise.

5   Players should work together so they arrive at the centre cone together.

Think about

- Planting your non-kicking foot at the side of the ball, just behind the line of the ball.

- Using the sole (bottom) of your foot to quickly drag the ball back, pulling it away from the defender.

- Pulling the foot back at speed to create the time and space to play it in another direction.

- The direction you want to turn away to – off to the side or a full 180° turn away from the defender.

- Accelerating away when you have created the space.

Figure 8.29 **Drill 25: Turning with opposition – the drag back**

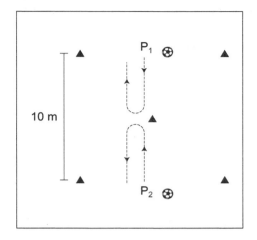

P   Player

⊗   Football

▲   Cones

-→ Direction of run/
    movement
    of player

Target

- Try to practise the technique with both feet.

Progression

- Use only one ball and six cones to create an attacker v defender situation.
  - Player 1 has possession of the ball within the grid and Player 2 acts as a defender.
  - Player 1 dribbles the ball into the centre of the grid and attempts to lose the defender by using a turn to create a space. Use a variety of different turns, be creative and accelerate away.
  - Player 1 can score by dribbling through one of the small target goals.

Figure 8.30 **Progression**

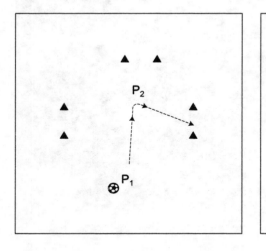

The Cruyff turn

DRILL 26: TURNING WITH OPPOSITION – THE CRUYFF TURN

Purpose

To develop your ability to turn the ball using the Cruyff method.

You need

5 cones

2 footballs

2 players

Activity

1   Players each have a ball and face each other in a 10 m × 10 m grid.

2   Both players dribble the ball to the middle of the grid, marked by a cone.

3   As they reach the cone, they turn away from each other using a Cruyff turn and dribble back to their starting point.

4   They have a few seconds' rest and then repeat the exercise.

5   Players should work together so they arrive at the centre cone together.

Think about

- Placing your standing foot past the ball as you approach the defender and drawing back the kicking foot as if to pass or shoot.

- Swinging the kicking foot over the ball using the inside of this foot to kick the ball behind the standing leg.

- Turning your body as quickly as possible to follow the ball in its new direction.

- Identifying the space which you want to go into and develop the flick accordingly.

Figure 8.31 **Drill 26: Turning with opposition – the Cruyff turn**

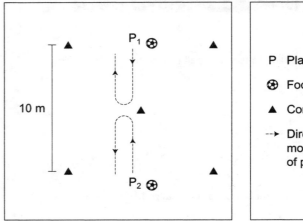

Target

- Try the same turn using your weaker foot.
- The more you practise the movement, the more fluid it will become.

Progression

- Use only one ball and six cones to create an attacker v defender situation.
  - Player 1 has possession of the ball within the grid and Player 2 acts as a defender.
  - Player 1 dribbles the ball into the centre of the grid and attempts to lose their marker by using a turn to create a space. Use a variety of different turns, be creative and accelerate away.
  - Player 1 can score by dribbling through one of the small target goals.

Shielding the ball

Players who have the technical ability and strength to shield the ball so that other players can come and support them are vital to their team, particularly when trying to keep possession. Having the ability to shield the ball is a combination of a good first touch accompanied by body strength to fend off other players.

Try the following practice with your team-mates to develop your technique for shielding the ball.

DRILL 27: HOLD THEM OFF AND LOOK FOR SUPPORT

Purpose

To develop your ability to shield the ball until support arrives.

You need

4 cones

1 football

3 players

Activity

1 Players 1 and 2 stand 1 m apart in the centre of a 10 m ×10 m grid. The server stands on the side of the grid.

2 The server plays the ball to the feet of Player 1.

3 Player 2 closes Player 1 down by moving in quickly.

4 Player 1 tries to shield the ball, holding off Player 2.

5 After 20 seconds, Player 1 can play the ball back to the server and collects a point.

6 Player 2 gets a point if they win the ball inside the 20 seconds.

7 Players alternate roles.

Figure 8.32 **Drill 27: Hold them off and look for support**

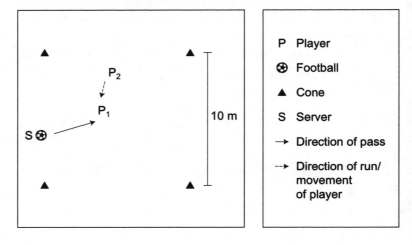

Think about

- Making sure you are the first to the ball.
- Leaning back slightly and bending your knees.
- Using your arms and body as a barrier to fend off the defender.
- Concentrating on a good first touch so the ball remains in close control.
- Keeping your body between the ball and the defender.

Target

- First player to reach five points after equal turns.

Progression

- Create a goal or target on the opposite side of the grid to the server.
  - The server plays the ball to Player 1 who shields the ball from Player 2, the defender.
  - After 20 seconds of shielding, Player 1 passes the ball back to the server who then takes a strike on goal.

Summary

This chapter has looked at a variety of different skills required, some fundamental to all positions, others more specific to you as a midfielder. Below are some top tips and reminders for these skills.

Passing
- When passing to your team-mate, try to pass to their foot which is furthest away from your opponent.
- When passing to a player in space, try to pass to the space just in front of them so they can collect the pass as they run, without having to break their stride.
- The safest and most accurate way of passing is to use the inside of the foot.
- When linking up with team-mates try to use the whole pitch, switching play and using the width, as this makes it difficult for the opposition to get close to the ball.
- Fast and safe passes will generally outplay the opposition.
- Remember, as soon as you have played a pass, get ready to take up a new position to receive another – pass and move.

Ball control
- Always try to receive the ball with an open body position, unless you are tightly marked.
- Move to meet the ball rather than wait for it.
- Try to use cushion control in tight situations when you do not want the ball to go far away from you.
- Use wedge control when the space is available to you, pushing the ball away from your opponent and into the space.
- Always have your toe slightly raised on your receiving foot, so that the ball doesn't bounce over your foot.
- Be prepared to use different surfaces to control the ball by getting into the line of the ball early.
- Try not to lose time by letting high balls bounce – get them down under control and use the time to your advantage.

Heading
- Defensive headers, close to your penalty area, should be headed high, long and wide.
- Attacking headers are about accuracy, so try to head them down for a team-mate or, if heading at the goal, down towards the ground to make it more difficult for a goalkeeper to save.
- Always attack the header, using the forehead, keeping your eyes open.

Shooting
- Be prepared to take every advantage you have to shoot, and accept that you will not score every time.
- Try to develop your accuracy when shooting, which is more important than power.
- Your head should be steady, with eyes on the ball.
- Strike through the ball, with your follow through in the line of the intended target.
- When shooting from an angle, always aim for the far post, across the goal. This way the keeper may be forced to parry your shot into the path of one of your team-mates.
- Low shots to the corner of the goal are the most difficult to save for a goalkeeper.
- Don't wait for the ball before shooting; waiting may give the opposition a chance to block your shot. Make your run into the path of the ball and shoot early.
- Be creative with your shooting, depending on the positioning of the goalkeeper – swerving, placing, chipping, lobbing, etc. Always have one last look up before shooting.

Dribbling
- When dribbling, if in tight situations, dribble slowly and have lots of touches of the ball – this is the best way to protect it.
- When dribbling in space, dribble at speed, sometimes kicking the ball ahead of you, but not too far as to lose possession.
- Your dribbling foot should be further away from your opponent than your other foot, keeping the ball closer to you.
- Try to keep your head up in order to see what is happening around you, rather than keeping your eyes fixed on the ball.

- When you are feinting to trick an opponent, trying to catch them off balance, do so while dribbling rather than when you are standing still.
- After going past your opponent, speed up your dribble or next move, to take full advantage of the situation.

Self testers

1 What is the difference between wedge control and cushion control?

2 Describe the Cruyff turn.

3 What are the main aims of a defensive header?

Action plan

1 Plan a seven-week training programme for yourself based around the seven areas highlighted in this chapter:

- passing
- ball control
- heading
- shooting
- dribbling
- turning
- shielding the ball.

2 Focus on each area for a week and choose some of the drills to practise the skills.

Chapter 9

Tactics and teamwork

THIS CHAPTER WILL:
- Highlight some tactics and support play that will help you to become an effective midfielder within a team.
- Provide drills and practices for you and your team-mates to try.
- Consider the decisions that midfielders need to make during a match, both in possession and out of possession.

Forcing the play

If a team is going to make the play of their opponents predictable, they must work together, communicate with each other and try to force their opponents into areas of the pitch that present less danger to them as a defending team. The individual roles for each midfielder will change depending on where the ball is and who the nearest player is.

These are the basic principles of defending when the ball is in the midfield area:

- **Pressure** – pressurizing the player on the ball (first midfielder).
- **Support** – supporting the pressurizing player (second midfielder).
- **Cover** – covering in the space behind the supporting player (third midfielder).

Forcing the play is generally the responsibility of the first midfielder who pressurizes the player on the ball. It is their decision and actions that will directly affect how successful a team is in forcing the play. For example, a first midfielder who does not pressurize quickly will allow their opponent the time to explore the space and possibly move into dangerous areas of the pitch. If you pressurize early, making progress as the ball travels to your opponent, you may be able to stop a player turning. If this happens, then you as the first midfielder have successfully forced the play. By stopping the ball being played forward, you allow your team-mates to get back behind the ball and offer the support and cover required for good defending.

There are times when a midfielder's body position and angle of approach when defending will dictate where the ball is played next. It will not always be possible for you as the first 'defender' to prevent the ball from being played forward, and you may even encourage a forward pass. For example, a midfielder working as the first 'defender' may allow an opponent to play the ball forward, down the line, rather than let them switch play across the pitch. This forward pass into a relatively restricted space is easier for their team-mates to defend against.

Figure 9.1 shows the position of three midfielders attempting to make play predictable, forcing the play across the pitch.

Figure 9.1 **Pressure, support and cover**

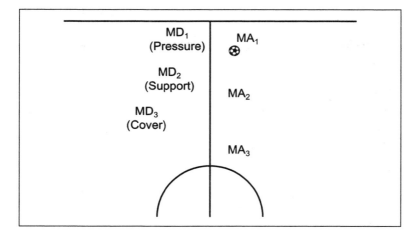

| MD | Midfielders—defending | MA | Midfielders—attacking | ⊕ | Football |

Top tip

Always remember, you should wait for the right time to make your tackle. The supporting midfielder and covering midfielder should constantly be giving information to the pressurizing player advising them of their supporting positions and encouraging them to force the play into less dangerous areas such as out to the wings or, better still, backwards.

Player-to-player marking

There are two defensive methods that a team may choose to use:

1 **Zonal.**
2 **Player to player.**

With both systems, the midfield players in the team will have specific roles, and good communication between all players is vital.

The zonal system involves all players taking responsibility for an area on the pitch. These are mainly the areas in and around their specific position, with a player marking opponents as they enter their 'zone'. The player-to-player marking method requires each player to take defensive responsibility for one of the opposition players.

Whichever system your team plays, good defending principles are required. You should always consider:

- **staying goal side**
- **staying close**
- **looking to intercept**
- **applying pressure**
- **looking to tackle when opportunity arises**
- **staying on your feet.**

Player-to-player marking is likely to be the system that gives you the greatest chance of intercepting the ball. Your starting position is relatively close to your opponent, and therefore your chance to intercept the ball will increase. However, if you get too close your opponent may take the opportunity to turn away from you, using their upper body and arms to hold you off. It is therefore important that you do not overcommit, or get too close. Your opponent needs to feel that you are close enough to tackle them if they turn or lose control of the ball – this is often called 'touch close'.

For you and your team-mates to practise the techniques and tactics of player-to-player marking, try the following practice.

DRILL 1: PLAYER-TO-PLAYER

Purpose

To develop player-to-player marking skills.

You need

10 cones
1 football
10 players
Set of bibs

Activity

Two teams play five-a-side on a 30 m × 40 m pitch (Teams A/B). Small target goals are placed at each end of the pitch. Every player has one opponent; they are responsible for marking and can only tackle that player and vice-versa. The practice develops player-to-player marking skills and exposes any player who is not working hard for their team.

Figure 9.2 **Drill 1: Player-to-player**

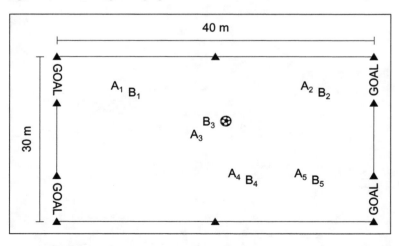

| A Team A player | B Team B player | ▲ Cone | ⊕ Football |

Key points

- Keep goal side.
- Try to anticipate your player's next move.
- Look to intercept.
- Try to prevent your player from turning.
- Pressure your opponent when they get the ball.

1 v 2 defending

There will be occasions in a game when your opponents will outnumber you. What you choose to do in this situation will have a direct impact on the success and outcome of the attack.

Unless one of your opponents loses control of the ball, you may find it difficult to win possession. However, there are good practices that you can follow to help your team. Ultimately, if you can slow down the attack you will be giving time for your team-mates to get back to support you and create a better defending situation which should ideally see pressure, support and cover in place.

Try this next drill to see how successful you and your team-mates are at holding up the attack.

DRILL 2: HOLD UP THE ATTACK

Purpose

To improve a midfield player's ability to delay an attack.

You need

6 cones

1 football

6 or more players

Activity

A group of midfielders is at one end of the grid and a group of attackers at the other. A midfielder passes the ball to one of the two attackers at the opposite end of the grid. After passing the ball, the midfielder tries to prevent the two attackers, Attacker 1 and Attacker 2, from reaching the end line. A second midfielder is released from the attackers' end to support the lone midfielder after ten seconds of the practice starting. The midfielder wins a point after tackling or forcing the attackers to lose possession.

Figure 9.3 **Drill 2: Hold up the attack**

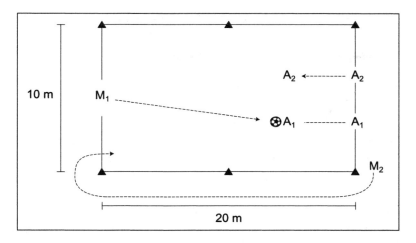

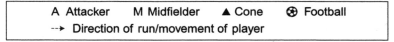

Key points

- Gain as much ground as possible after making your pass.
- Slow down when 'touching distance' away from your attacker.
- Adopt a good defensive position, side on, with knees bent.
- Try to make play predictable.
- Keep both of the attackers in your view at all times.
- Can you hold up the attack until the second midfielder assists you?

Progression

- Develop the practice to a 2 v 2 defending drill (see p. 192).

2 v 2 defending

Although 2 v 2 situations are not ideal for defending teams, they should be less dangerous than the 1 v 2 situations referred to on p. 190. Once again, there are some fundamental defending principles that you and your team-mates should follow which will lead to effective defending in midfield areas. The principles need to be practised on a regular basis and your coach should be encouraged to work on defending practices and positioning just as much as the 'more popular' attacking and shooting drills.

Earlier in the chapter we referred to the pressure, support and cover roles provided by three players in a defending situation. As a midfield player you may find yourself defending in 2 v 2 situations. This will require you and your team-mate to slightly modify the pressure, support and cover principles referred to when there are three defending midfield players available.

The next drill provides you with a chance to develop your 2 v 2 defensive techniques, providing pressure, support and cover to cope with the attack.

DRILL 3: PRESSURE, SUPPORT AND COVER

Purpose

To improve defensive positioning in 2 v 2 situations.

You need

6 cones
1 football
Minimum of 4 players

Activity

Four players work in a grid 10 m × 20 m. Two players represent attackers and start at one end. The other two players are defending and start at the opposite end of the grid. The two attackers slowly dribble the ball forward, passing the ball between them. The two midfielders slowly retreat, with an emphasis on keeping their correct defensive positions. There is no tackling in the practice.

Figure 9.4 **Drill 3: Pressure, support and cover**

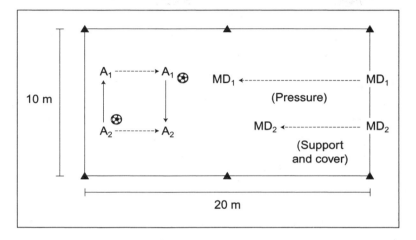

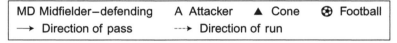

Key points

- Players need to adjust their defensive position quickly as the ball is passed between the attackers – you should do this as the ball is travelling.
- The supporting midfielder needs to communicate to the pressurizing midfielder.
- The supporting/covering midfielder should always be in a position to cover the pressurizing midfielder and mark their own attacker.

Progression

- Increase the speed of the practice.
- Make the practice competitive, and introduce tackling.

Pressurizing opponents

Changeover of possession occurs in the midfield areas of the pitch more than in any other area. It is therefore vital that you have the stamina and technique to close players down as the 'first defender', delaying the attack and enabling your team to get players behind the ball. A good practice to work on for you and your coach to improve this is the '1 v 3 switch grid' drill.

DRILL 4: SWITCH GRIDS

Purpose

To practise putting pressure on opponents.

You need

6 cones for 2 grids
2 footballs
Minimum of 8 players

Activity

Four players are in each grid, with one football per group. The players play one and two touch football among themselves. Each player has a number between 1 to 4 in each team (yellow/red teams). On the coach's start, the coach calls out a number between 1 to 4 and that player immediately runs to the other grid to try to win the ball in a 1 v 3 situation. The first player to win the ball is awarded a point for their team.

Key points

- Good defensive technique.
- Make ground up as quickly as possible.
- Try to intercept the ball.
- Stay on your feet.
- Wait for the right time to tackle.
- Try to face the play and get the ball into tight situations.

Figure 9.5 **Drill 4: Switch grids**

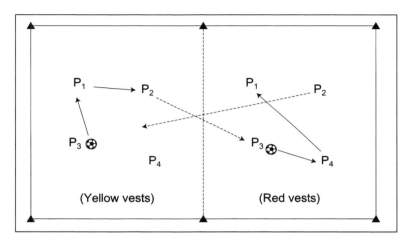

P Player   ▲ Cone   ⊕ Football

The defensive shape of the midfield

The team formations and systems used by most teams have been highlighted on pages 10–25. Each of the systems, whether there are three, four or five players in midfield, provides some form of balance and positional team shape to counter different attacking situations.

The following drills will help you and your midfield team-mates to develop your defensive shape and balance, and can be modified to suit different formations. The drills provide you and your coach with the opportunity to put into practice some of the key defending principles that midfield players need to practise as a team.

It is important to recognize that the pattern of play is forever changing and that your individual movement and role changes with every pass made. Concentration and team communication are crucial.

DRILL 5: KEEP THE SHAPE (FULL WIDTH)

Purpose

To improve the defensive shape of the midfield players.

You need

Half of the pitch
Minimum 12 outfield players
Goalkeeper and several footballs

Activity

A line is marked with cones dividing the playing area in half. Four midfielders are in the defending half with four attackers on the end line. The attackers move towards the midfielders with the ball, attacking the end line. Their aim is to score a goal by stopping the ball on the end line. If they score, they remain as attackers. If they do not score and lose possession, they change roles with the midfield defenders who then join the attacking group of players. Attackers A5, A6, A7 and A8

Figure 9.6 **Drill 5: Keep the shape**

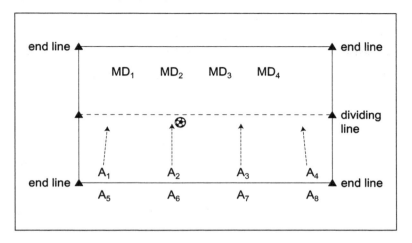

A Attacker   MD Midfielder defending   ▲ Cone   ⊗ Football
--→ Direction of run

join in the practice by rotating with other groups after approximately 5 minutes.

Key points

- The four players should be spread evenly across the pitch.
- Depending on the position of the ball, the closest midfielder should pressurize the player on the ball. The 'second midfielder' should add support with the other midfielders providing cover and balance to the defensive unit.
- Communication from players behind the pressurizing midfielder advising the midfielder where to force the attacker, inside, down the line, etc.
- Position of back four players should be changing in relation to the position of the ball.

Figure 9.7 **The defensive shape of the midfield when the ball is in a wide position**

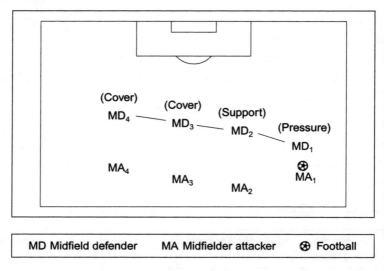

MD Midfield defender　　MA Midfielder attacker　　⊕ Football

Figure 9.8 **The defensive shape of the midfield when the ball is in a central position**

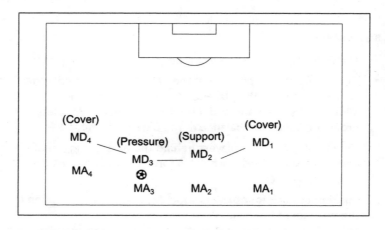

MD Midfield defender　　MA Midfielder attacker　　⊕ Football

Defending as a team

Closing down and defending as a team is essential if your team wants to win back possession from the opposition. To be effective, players need to be prepared to work hard in all positions. Any part of the game that requires teamwork and tactics needs to be practised so that the team is organized, with each player knowing their role and having an understanding between each other.

Defending and regaining possession can be physically quite demanding and one thing that you may soon realize is how important it is not to give possession away easily. The better your team is at keeping possession, the less defending your team will have to do.

There are two options your team can adopt as a defensive tactic: high pressure and low pressure.

High pressure

If teams choose to play with high pressure, your coach will be encouraging you and your team-mates to try to win the ball back as close to the opponent's goal as possible. This involves all players in your team and requires a high work rate. You need to reduce the time and space your opponent's have on the ball and make the play as predictable as possible. Denying the opposition space is a principle of good defensive play.

If a defending team manages to win the ball back high up the pitch, an advantage they have is that they can quickly attack their opponent's goal after regaining possession. This tactic is likely to be used by a team that is losing with only a few minutes of the game remaining, but it can be used at any time by a team with fit, hard-working players.

Midfield players will play their part with this defensive tactic, taking responsibility for the opposition's midfield players, preventing them from having time on the ball. As a midfield player you should be passing information on to your strikers who will be defending in front of you and will rely on good communication.

Low pressure

A defence that has players drop back and retreat after losing possession is operating a low pressure form of defending. With this system, whoever is closest to the attacking player when possession is lost will try to delay the opponent's attack. This will allow other players in the defending team to get behind the ball and reform the defence. The space that the players are defending is a reduced one, compared to the space with a high-pressure system. The retreating players should be aiming to defend with a compact team shape.

As soon as the ball is lost, all players retreat and get back behind the ball. The first defender 'jockeys' the opponent to create time for other players to get back into their defensive position. Whenever the defending team regains possession, the retreating stops and, at this point, it is common for a defending team to launch some kind of counter-attack. With the space available in front of them this can be very effective.

Top tip

As with all good defending teams, whatever tactic or style you are adopting you need to be organized and communicate well with each other throughout a match.

Supporting play

As a midfielder you will be expected to get forward and support the player on the ball. Sometimes this support will be from behind or to the side as a holding midfield player. At other times, as an attacking midfielder, you may need to offer support by getting alongside or in front of the player in possession. Making forward runs is an exciting and important role for midfielders to perform. If you watch top teams and top players perform you will see how often midfield players get forward to join the attack. Frank Lampard at England team Chelsea is a great example of this type of midfielder. It is no coincidence that, as a result of getting forward and supporting the attack, Frank Lampard ended the 2005/06 season as the club's top goal scorer. The midfielder getting forward can be decisive in terms of creating the extra player for a 2 v 1 situation and a numerical advantage.

The overlap

A midfield player who chooses to run past the player in possession into the forward space is making an overlapping run. The player in possession is likely to be facing the opponent's goal with their head up and an awareness of what is happening around them. The overlapping player will normally call for the ball as they run past the player in possession. A 2 v 1 advantage for the attacking team created by this run is difficult to defend against.

DRILL 6: AN OVERLAPPING RUN

Figure 9.9 **Drill 6: An overlapping run**

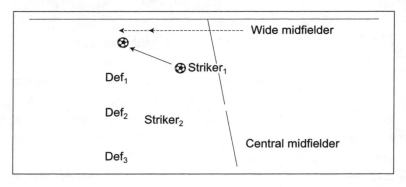

Def Defender	⊕ Football	--→ Direction of run
→ Direction of pass		

Key points

- Strikers create the space for the overlap.
- Quality of the pass for the wide midfielder to receive.
- Timing and angle of run of the wide midfielder.
- Wide midfielder's next move – cross, shot or pass?
- Striker cuts inside if overlapping run is blocked.

DRILL 7: PASS AND OVERLAP

Purpose

To encourage midfielders to overlap after making a pass.

You need

10 cones
Minimum six players
1 football

Activity

Two groups of players face each other at opposite ends of a 10 m x 20 m grid. Player 1 passes the ball through the two centre cones to the players at the opposite end of the grid. After making the pass Player 1 then sprints around the side cone, representing an overlapping run, and joins the other group.

Figure 9.10 **Drill 7: Pass and overlap**

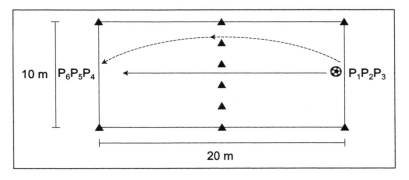

Key points

- Passes should be kept on the ground.
- One-touch play whenever possible.
- Purposeful and determined overlapping run.
- Try to keep the practice continuous.

Progression

A player moves into the centre of the grid to receive a pass and plays a pass into the path of the overlapping player.

Third man running

In many ways 'third man running' is similar to the overlap. It is a forward run and is based on a player supporting their team in possession. The only real difference is that it involves three, rather than two, players. A player passes the ball to a holding player, such as a central striker facing his or her own goal. The ball is then played back to a midfielder. The player who has made the first pass will have set off on an attacking forward run, anticipating the next pass to be a forward one. The midfield player who receives the lay back, passes the ball to this player. The run needs to be purposeful and determined and is an effective tactic for good forward play. It can also see a numerical advantage for the attacking team. The following practice encourages support play with third man runs.

DRILL 8: THIRD MAN RUNNING

Purpose

To encourage players to make third man runs.

You need

6 cones
Up to 8 players
1 football

Activity

In a 10 m × 20 m grid, six players face each other at opposite ends of the grid. Two players are placed in the centre of the grid to receive passes. Player 1 passes the ball to Player 7 and sprints forward, following their pass. Players 7 plays a short pass to Player 8 who then plays the ball into the path of Player 1 who collects and makes a short pass to Player 4 before joining the back of the queue.

Figure 9.11 **Drill 8: Third man running**

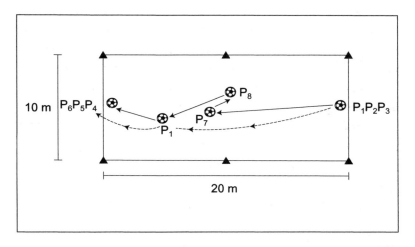

P Player	▲ Cone	⊕ Football	→ Direction of pass
--→ Direction of run			

Key points

- Quality of initial pass.
- Quality of short pass in the centre of the grid.
- Purposeful and determined 'third man run'.
- Timing of run and timing of pass.

Blind-side runs

Another forward run which you should be encouraged to make is a 'blind-side run'. It also supports the attack and can be a useful tactic in terms of creating goal-scoring opportunities. If, for example, you made this type of run on the wide right of midfield, the ball is likely to be on the left side of the pitch in a reasonably advanced position, with your team in possession. Teams defending with the ball on one side of the pitch can often watch the ball, rather than what is going on around them. If this situation is happening, you can try to exploit the space behind the last defender by making a blind-side run down the right side.

For this to be effective, the secret is for the run to be unnoticed, as late as possible, and out of the vision of the defenders. However, the attacking team in possession needs to be able to see the run that you have made, in order to make the pass. Hand signals can be used to make your team aware of your run without drawing attention to yourself and allowing the defending team to readjust their position.

A blind-side run by a wide midfielder
Key points

- Attacking team creates the space.
- Quality of the pass into the space behind the defenders.
- Timing and angle of run of the wide midfielder.
- Quality of pass, cross or shot of the wide midfielder.

Figure 9.12 **Diagram showing a blind-side run**

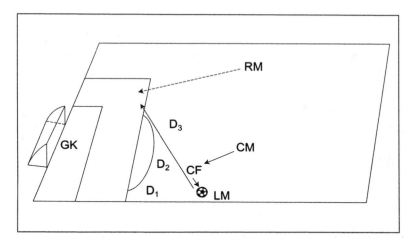

| ⊕ Football   --▸ Direction of run   → Direction of pass   D Defender |
| CF Centre forward   CM Central midfielder   LM Left midfielder |
| RM Wide right midfielder |

The wall-pass

The 'give and go', or wall-pass as it is commonly known, is a popular pass and relies on a supporting run from the player making the initial pass. It is used all over the pitch, but none more so than in the midfield areas. It allows a player in possession to attack and get past an opponent by creating a numerical advantage using a supporting team-mate. It can also be used as a tactic to keep possession in tight areas as well as a way to move the ball across the pitch.

DRILL 9: GIVE AND GO

Purpose

To develop a midfielder's technique to play the wall-pass.

You need

5 cones
Minimum of 4 players
1 football

Activity

A small group of players stands in pairs at one end of a 10 m × 25 m grid. A cone is placed in the centre of this playing area. One of the players starts the practice by dribbling from the end line towards the centre of the grid. As the player gets nearer to the centre cone, they play a one-two, or wall-pass, with Player 2 around the cone and then continue to dribble through to the end line. The next pair of players continues the practice.

Key points

- Passes should be firm and accurate.
- The pass can be made with the inside or outside of the foot.
- Disguising the pass can make the move more effective.
- Try to pass the ball into your team-mate's run so they can play first time.

Figure 9.13 **Drill 9: Give and go**

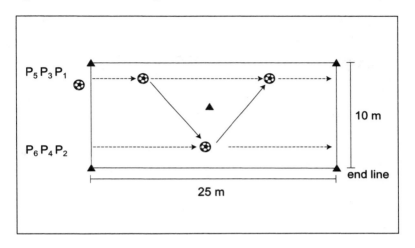

- Try to keep the pass on the ground.
- Make the extra player count!

Progression

- Rather than use the cone to represent a defender/opponent, introduce a player who can tackle to make the drill more realistic.
- Player in possession then has the option of either using the wall-pass or dribbling to beat the opponent and reach the end line.
- Introduce a second defender 10m down the grid.

Cross-over runs

The purpose of making supporting runs is to receive the ball in space. However, there are occasions when you make a run and you don't want to receive the ball. You actually want to create space for other players to receive the ball, which is the purpose of cross-over runs.

Cross-over runs need to be rehearsed and practised on the training ground so that players understand each other's signals.

Strikers often make these runs, and it is not uncommon for an attacking midfielder to exploit the space created by a cross-over run. To create space for a team-mate, your run will normally be at an angle and slightly towards the player in possession. Make a deliberate and loud call for the ball, so that the defender follows your run. When this happens it creates a space for another player to run in to receive the pass.

Cross-over run

Key points

- Striker's awareness of space.
- Quality and purpose of striker's run.
- Vision of central midfielder to see the pass.
- Quality of pass.
- Timing and angle of run by attacking midfielder.
- End product from attacking midfielder – pass, cross or shot?

Figure 9.14 **Cross-over run**

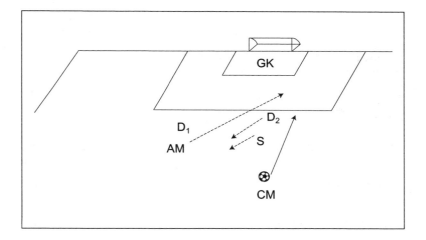

⊕ Football --► Direction of run → Direction of pass D Defender
S Striker   CM Central midfielder   AM Attacking midfielder

Keeping possession

Whether you are a holding, attacking or wide midfield player it is extremely important that you have a good passing technique in order to keep possession for your team. You will often find yourself in possession and under pressure from opponents. It is the ability that a player has to cope with this pressure, yet still keep possession for their team, that makes them effective midfield players.

Practising passing when unopposed is good for developing technique, but practices also need to take place when a player is put under pressure to really test the technique. The following three practices are all aimed at developing passing skills under pressure. They encourage passing and moving, creating angles, disguising passes and looking up before passing.

DRILL 10: 3 V 1 PASSING UNDER PRESSURE

Purpose

To develop passing skills in order to keep posession.

You need

4 cones
1 football
4 players

Activity

Four players take part in this practice – three midfield players and one defender. The midfield players try to keep possession while being put under pressure from the defender. Midfield players are awarded a point for every five consecutive passes.

Key points

• **The two supporting midfield players must try to offer support to the player in possession.**

Figure 9.15 **Drill 10: 3 v 1 passing under pressure**

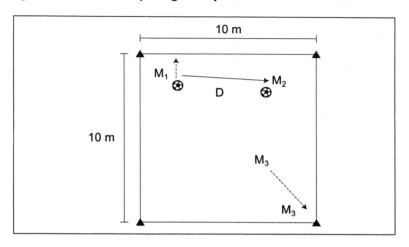

M Midfield player	D Defender	▲ Cone	⊕ Football
→ Direction of pass	---→ Direction of run		

- The support should be deep and wide.
- Disguise passes to mislead the defender.
- High tempo passes.
- Pass and move.

Progression

- Increase the size of grid to 20 m × 20 m.
- Play 5 v 2.
- Limit the passes to two-touch.

DRILL 11: COUNT THE PASSES

Purpose

To improve the midfield player's technical ability to make short accurate passes.

You need

4 cones

1 football

2 bibs

10 players

Activity

The practice takes place in a 20 m × 20 m grid. There are two defenders within the grid. The outfield players take up a position on the outside of the grid and keep possession. They are only allowed two touches. The

Figure 9.16 **Drill 11: Count the passes**

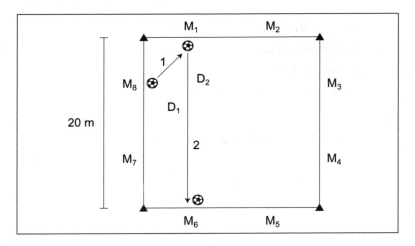

M Midfield player	D Defenders	▲ Cone	⊕ Football
→ Direction of pass			

players receive a point for every ten consecutive passes and an additional point if they can pass the ball between the two defenders. If a player loses possession, they swap with a defender.

Key points

- Disguise the pass – use different parts of the foot to make a pass.
- Accuracy and timing.
- Look up before passing.
- Weight of the pass.

DRILL 12: SEQUENCE PASSING

Purpose

To encourage midfield players to pass and move and improve their first-time passing.

You will need

4 cones

1 football

8 players

Activity

Eight players work in a 20 m × 20 m grid. Each player is allocated a number. Players pass the ball first time, through the number sequence – 1 to 2, 2 to 3 and so on. The coach can reverse this at any time so 8 passes to 7, 7 to 6 and so on.

Figure 9.17 **Drill 12: Sequence passing**

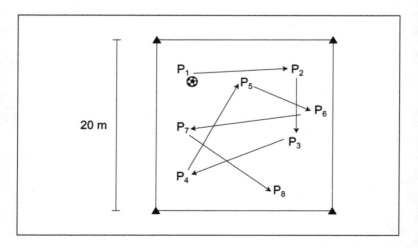

P Player   ▲ Cone   ⊕ Football   → Direction of pass

Key points

- Players due to receive the ball should shout out their number.
- Receiving players should move into a good position ready to receive the pass.
- Receiving players should look around before receiving their pass so that they know where their next pass is to go.
- Make confident, firm passes.
- Pass and move.

Progression

- A defender can be introduced to increase the pressure on the passing players.

Passing through the midfield

Although there are no specific lines across a pitch marking thirds, there are general terms that your coach may use to describe the playing areas. These are the defensive third, midfield third and attacking third. At times your team may build up an attack by playing or passing through each third. It is generally accepted that this is an attractive way of playing the game. Teams playing this way need players who are comfortable in possession, good passers of the ball and players who are prepared to work hard off the ball to make the vital runs into space.

Goalkeepers will look to throw the ball out to full-backs rather than kicking it up the pitch, because the latter only results in a 50:50 chance of a team keeping possession. Once the defenders receive the ball from the goalkeeper, they will look to pass the ball through the midfield.

As a midfield player you will need to be able to pass and move, make attacking runs, deliver accurate passes, switch play across the pitch into space and have excellent close control.

The following practice can be used by your team to practise passing through the midfield to build up your attack.

DRILL 13: PASSING THROUGH THE MIDFIELD

Purpose

To encourage passing and support play.

You need

8 cones

2 goals

14 players

Activity

Two teams play against each other in a 20 m × 40 m area, seven-a-side, including two goalkeepers (Team A and Team B). Players are restricted to certain thirds. The main condition of the game is that the attacking play has to go through the midfield (middle zone). When a player makes a pass into the next third they can follow their pass to make an extra player and create a 3 v 2 situation. Their marker cannot follow them into the next third.

Figure 9.18 **Drill 13: Passing through the midfield**

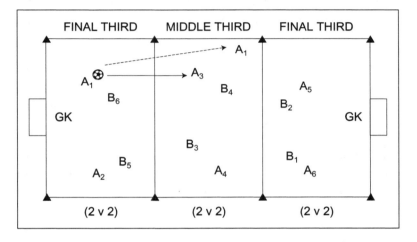

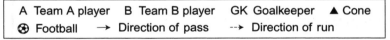

Key points

- Make short rather than long passes.
- Players must support their forward pass.
- Timing of runs to make use of extra player.
- Good receiving skill, particularly players in middle third.

Switching play in midfield

Switching play can take place anywhere on the pitch by any player. As a midfielder you should understand the reasons why a switch of play can be an advantage to your team. One of the most common times that a switch of play occurs is when a team is attacking down one flank and the forward pass is blocked, either by lack of space or by facing too many defenders. A good tactic is to think about passing the ball infield to a central midfield player who can then play across the pitch. By playing a quick long ball to the other wing you are changing the focus of the play. You may catch out your opponents who may not be organized and ready to deal with the situation.

Top tip

If you are going to switch play, make it happen fast before the opportunity has gone, and try to pass the ball into the space for your team-mate to run onto.

The practice below assists you and your fellow midfielders to practise switching the play across the middle third concentrating on distance of support and accuracy of pass.

DRILL 14: SWITCHING PLAY IN THE MIDDLE THIRD (WARM-UP)

Purpose

To develop the technical ability to hit long accurate passes.

You need

4 cones

1 football

8 players

Activity

To switch play, midfield players need the technical ability to hit accurate long passes. Players hit passes to any corner and then follow the ball to a new corner. Players can pass along the sides of the grid or diagonally across the grid.

Figure 9.19 **Drill 14: Switching play in the middle third (warm-up)**

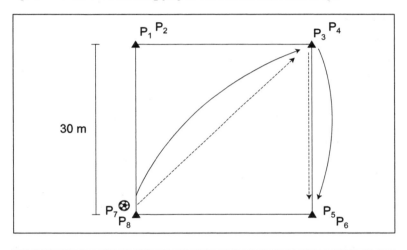

Key points

- Good passing technique.
- Lofted pass technique (see p. 95).
- Low driven pass technique (see p. 94).

DRILL 15: SWITCHING PLAY IN THE MIDDLE THIRD

Purpose

To develop the accuracy of long passing in the middle third of the pitch.

You need

1 football
5 players
One-third of a pitch

Activity

Four midfield players and a striker are positioned within the middle third of the pitch – approximately 30 m × 50 m. Player 1, a wide midfield player, starts with the ball and passes to Player 2. Player 2 then plays a long diagonal pass to Player 5, another wide midfielder. Player 3, a striker, makes a run to receive the ball from Player 5. Player 3 then lays

Figure 9.20 **Drill 15: Switching play in the middle third**

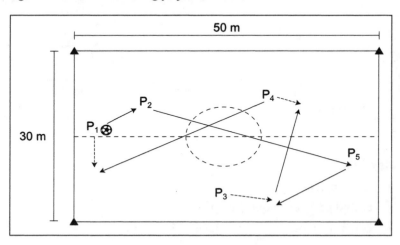

P Player   ▲ Cone   ⊕ Football   → Direction of pass
--→ Direction of run

the ball back to Player 4 who has offered support. Player 4 then plays a long diagonal pass to Player 1 for the practice to start again.

Key points

- After making your pass, take up a new supporting position.
- Distance between each midfield player – don't get too close.
- Try to play the ball into the path of the wide midfielder (P1/P5) to run onto.
- Midfield players should try making the long passes with both their right and left feet.

Progression

- Introduce two defenders to put some pressure on the passing sequence but do not allow them to tackle.

Using width in attacking situations

| Quote | 'I would tell a wide midfielder to be positive, clever, try crosses from different angles and let the thing that you do best be the last thing you do as this is what the full-back will remember.' (Peter Taylor) |

When most teams attack you will normally see at least one player in the team occupy a wide position. This is not always a winger, it may be a wide midfielder, wingback or even an overlapping full-back.

Players in central midfield positions are always looking to play accurate and effective passes, particularly to wide players. Good midfield players should have the technical ability, and the vision from playing with their heads up, to make accurate wide passes.

There are several advantages to playing with a wide player:

- If the ball is out wide, then defenders have to come out of the central areas of the pitch, which opens up the space in the middle areas and stretches the defence.

- Moving defenders out of the central areas allows the wide players, who are crossing the ball, the space to aim their crosses.

- If defenders do not come out of the central areas then the wide players can attack the space and progress towards the penalty area.

- Wide players with space to cross the ball can develop a range of crosses that are difficult to defend against. An early cross into the space behind the defenders and crosses pulled back from the by-line are particularly difficult to defend against.

The practice opposite is a conditioned game involving 16 players and encourages teams to look to play the ball wide as early as possible.

DRILL 16: ATTACK WITH WIDTH

Purpose

To encourage the use of wide midfield players when building attacks.

You need

Approximately 20 cones
2 goals
14 players plus 2 goalkeepers

Activity

This practice takes place in half a pitch, approximately 30 m × 50 m and involves 16 players. Two teams play 5 v 5 in the middle channel and two wide midfield players are positioned in each wide channel. The wide players play for whichever team is in possession. Players in the middle channel are restricted to this area and the wide players restricted to the wide channels. Players in the middle channel can only score after the ball

Figure 9.21 **Drill 16: Attack with width**

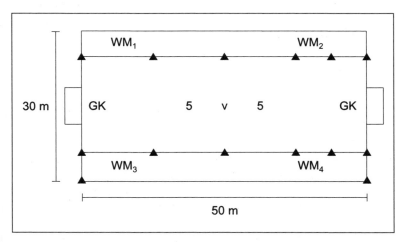

WM   Wide midfielder   GK   Goalkeeper

has been played out to one of the four wide midfielders who then look to cross the ball for the attacking team.

Key points

- Central players should look to get the ball out wide as soon as possible using both wide channels.

- Wide players should vary the crosses to the front and back post, including low and hard crosses and high lofted crosses to the back post.

- Central players should look to create space using good turning techniques and play one or two touch whenever possible.

- Wide players should be encouraged to link up play and set up crosses for each other.

- Central players should concentrate on timing their runs into the penalty area (late runs are more difficult to defend against).

Midfield passing options

A midfield player, particularly a central midfield player, is likely to make the most number of passes for their team. How well the team plays will be affected by the accuracy of these passes. It is therefore essential that midfield players have a good passing technique for both short- and long-range passes. They also need to be able to play one-touch and two-touch passes as the midfield area often has little space to play in. The next drill creates a range of passes designed for central midfield players to practise.

DRILL 17: FIND THE PLAYER

Purpose

To develop a midfield player's ability to deliver a range of accurate passes.

You need

4 cones
Several footballs
9 players plus a coach
Different vests

Activity

Two central midfield players exchange passes in a small grid of 10 m × 20 marked out within half a pitch. On the coach's command, one of the central midfield players makes a pass to the player selected by the coach. Target players are placed in different areas of the pitch. Three players wear different coloured bibs and interchange after each pass, so the central midfielder needs to look where they are before making a pass. A point is awarded for each successful pass.

Figure 9.22 **Drill 17: Find the Player**

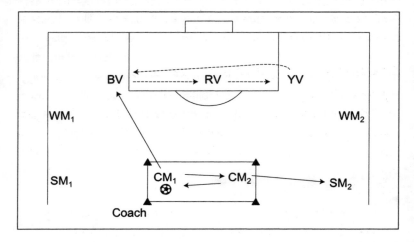

Players BV Blue vest RV Red vest YV Yellow vest
WM Wide midfielder SM Supporting midfielder
CM Centre midfielder ⊕ Football ▲ Cones

Key points

- Player in possession, when coach calls out a player, plays the pass.
- Look up before passing.
- Play 'two touch' – one to set up and one to pass.
- Play first time if the situation allows.
- Concentrate on accuracy and technique.

Progression

- A defender is introduced to the small grid and puts pressure on the two central midfield players without actually tackling.
- Vary the position of the target players to increase distances of long-range passes.

Statistic

40% of all goals scored result from a cross. Fast, low crosses produce more goals than any other type of cross.

Crossing using wide players

We have already referred to the benefits of using width in attack (p. 224) with players in a good position to cross the ball. Crosses make goals, so therefore should be practised to make them effective. It is often a wide midfield player who makes the cross into the penalty area, though where the player actually crosses the ball will determine how successful the outcome is:

- Too near the goalkeeper and they are likely to collect the ball.
- The ball is likely to be cleared if it doesn't get over the first defender.
- Possession may be lost if the cross is too deep.
- If the ball is cut back from the by-line into the path of an advancing striker or midfield player it is likely to result in a strike on goal.

Quote | 'If the right winger is taking on the left-back, I would expect the left winger to be in the box.' (Peter Taylor)

Top tip

Practise crossing the ball with both feet so that, when the situation arises, you are confident of making a good cross. This is better than checking back on to your preferred foot allowing time for more defenders to get back.

The following practice will help midfield players improve their crossing technique and at the same time create striking options for players advancing into the penalty area.

DRILL 18: TWO TO CROSS

Purpose

Improve crossing technique of wide midfield players.

You need

4 cones

Several footballs

2 goals

10 players including 2 goalkeepers

Activity

Four players with a ball each are positioned at each corner of an area approximately 40 m × 50 m. Two goals are protected by two goal-keepers. Four other midfield players are positioned in a grid 10 m × 10 m in the centre of the pitch. Each player in the central grid is given a number 1 to 4. Players on each corner are also given a number between 1 and 4. When the coach calls out a number, that player sprints from the central grid to the corner of the corresponding number and the two players interchange passes. They then cross the ball into the penalty area. The three players left in the central grid become attackers and try to convert the cross by scoring past the goalkeeper.

Key points

* **Players crossing the ball should vary their crosses to the near and far post and attempt to play both low and hard crosses as well as lofted crosses.**
* **Players should try to cross with both right and left feet.**

Figure 9.23 **Drill 18: Two to cross**

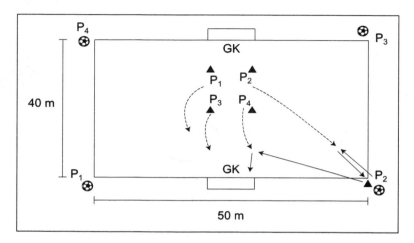

- Quality of lay off should allow the player crossing to play a first-time cross.

- Players crossing the ball should look up to see where the attackers are before making the cross.

- Players making runs from the central grid should make different runs to different parts of the penalty area and think about the timing of the run.

Progression

- A defender is introduced to each penalty area to work with the goalkeeper to defend the crosses.

- Crosses will need to be more accurate and kept away from the defender and goalkeeper.

Figure 9.24 **Where to hit the crosses from the by-line**

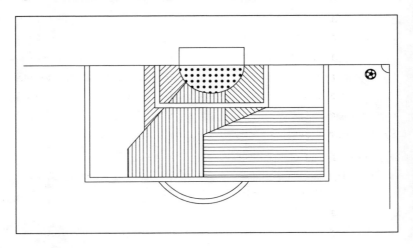

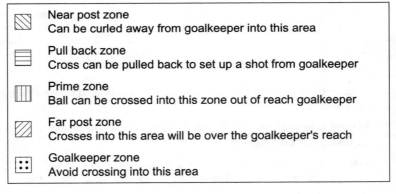

Near post zone
Can be curled away from goalkeeper into this area

Pull back zone
Cross can be pulled back to set up a shot from goalkeeper

Prime zone
Ball can be crossed into this zone out of reach goalkeeper

Far post zone
Crosses into this area will be over the goalkeeper's reach

Goalkeeper zone
Avoid crossing into this area

Counter-attacking from midfield

There are many different ways that a side will build up an attack, and as a midfielder you will often be the starting point of the attack. One of the most exciting forms of attack is the counter-attack and midfield players have a key role in this. It is a match winning tactic, and British sides like Arsenal and Manchester United are experts at it. In simple terms it involves turning defensive play into attack with a fast incisive break. Features of a fast counter-attack are:

- One quick short pass followed by a long pass, or simply a long pass.
- Players supporting their team-mates quickly.
- Any space in front of a player is attacked.
- Forward runs are diagonal rather than straight to avoid running offside.
- Players have good technique and are physically fit and fast.

The following two practices will help to develop your team's ability to counter-attack quickly after regaining possession. The first practice is relatively unopposed and gets your central midfield players into the habit of playing the ball out of the congested areas as quickly as possible and for at least one central midfield player to support the fast break. The second practice involves two teams and is a more realistic game situation.

DRILL 19: COUNTER-ATTACK 1

Purpose

To develop attacking skills from midfield.

You need

6 cones

Several footballs

Minimum of 8 players including goalkeeper

1 goal

Bibs

Activity

Two teams play 2 v 2 in a small grid 15 m × 15 m. Team B starts in possession. As soon as Team A wins possession they play the ball out to one of the wide midfield players who is restricted to a wide channel. The wide midfielder then plays first time up to a striker who then lays the ball back to one of the advancing midfield players from Team A to shoot on goal. Team B players must remain in the starting grid.

Key points

- Team regaining possession should play the ball wide as early as possible.
- Player in possession should turn away from other players to find the space to make the pass.
- The pass should be played on the ground allowing the wide midfielder to play the first-time pass up to the striker.
- The breaking midfield player should sprint from the grid to support the striker.
- Quality of lay off should allow the midfield player to shoot first time.

Figure 9.25 **Drill 19: Counter-attack 1**

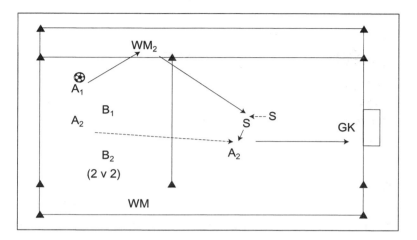

A Team A player	B Team B player	GK Goalkeeper	S Striker

⊕ Football → Direction of pass or shot ⇢ Direction of run
WM Wide midfielder

Progression

- Introduce a time limit on possession of ten seconds to produce a shot on goal from playing up to the striker.

DRILL 20: COUNTER-ATTACK 2

Purpose

To develop counter-attacking skills from midfield.

You need

Approximately 20 cones

2 goals

2 goalkeepers

12 outfield players

Bibs

Footballs

Activity

The practice starts with the coach feeding the ball into one of the midfield teams who keeps the ball for at least three passes. They can use the floating player to assist them. After playing three passes one of the midfield players plays a pass up to the striker in the central end zone. The striker plays the ball out wide to one of the wide midfield players who crosses the ball into the penalty area for a 1 v 1 situation on goal. One of the midfield players whose team is in possession can break forward to support the striker and create a 2 v 1 situation. If the defending team wins the ball in this 2 v 1 situation, they can immediately look for their striker and attack on goal, using a supporting midfielder to create a 2 v 1 situation at the other end of the pitch.

Key points

- Look to pass early up to strikers – midfield player needs good vision to see the pass.
- Quality of pass to striker will enable a first-time lay off to wide midfielder.
- Wide midfielder should look up before crossing.

Figure 9.26 **Drill 20: Counter-attack 2**

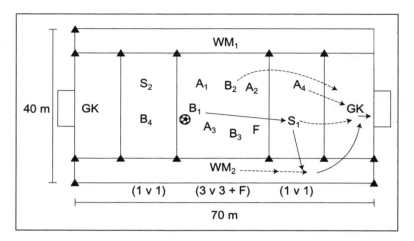

A Team A player B Team B player GK Goalkeeper ▲ Cone
⊕ Football → Direction of pass or shot ⇢ Direction of run
WM Wide midfielder F Floater S Striker

- Good communications between all attacking players.
- Wide midfielder on opposite channel tracks the far post.

Progression

- Introduce a time limit on possession of, say, ten seconds to produce a shot on goal from playing up to the striker.

Set plays

Statistic

There are, on average, 110 set piece situations per game (corners, throw-ins, free kicks, goal kicks).

Midfield players are likely to be involved in many set plays, and therefore need to concentrate and carry out their task as quickly and accurately as possible. Table 9.1 outlines the tasks you will need to think about as a midfield player when you are in a **defensive** situation.

Table 9.1 **Defensive situation**

Throw-ins	Corner kicks	Free kicks
Marking opposing midfield players.	Marking opposing players, not necessarily your opposing midfield player.	Are you a player in the wall, or are you marking a player?
Tracking the runs of opposing midfield players.	Communicating with your team-mates.	Are you charging the ball down as soon as the kick is taken?
Communicating with players in your team.	Listening to commands from your goalkeeper.	Listening to commands from the goalkeeper.
Concentrating as soon as the ball goes out, so you are ready for when it comes back into play.	Concentrating as soon as the ball goes out, so you are ready when it comes back into play.	Concentrating as soon as the free kick is awarded so a quick free kick does not catch you off guard.
If you gain possession, where is your next pass, so that your team keep possession?	If you gain possession, can you start a counter-attack?	If you are a player in the wall or charging the ball down, be brave and be prepared to get hurt. Do not turn your back on the ball.

Midfield players also need to react quickly and carry out their role in different **attacking** set plays. Table 9.2 outlines the tasks for this.

Table 9.2 **Attacking situations**

Throw-ins	Corner kicks	Free kicks
Movement away from ball and then show for the throw – lose your marker.	Movement at corners – does your team have a specific plan which involves you making a certain run?	Are you taking the kick?
If the thrower already has two options, you may not need to get involved in the throw-in, but concentrate on supporting the player who receives the throw.	Are you the corner taker?	Is the free kick going to be delivered as part of rehearsed practice?
Are you taking the throw-in?	Is a quick short corner an option?	Do you have a specific role to play in the free kick (e.g. dummy run)?
Is there a quick throw-in which catches out your opponents?	If you take the corner, are you delivering it away from the goalkeeper?	Are you a holding midfield player and not necessarily involved? If so you may need to be prepared to stop any counter-attack.
Are you looking to throw the ball long, into the penalty area – if so you may need to wait for your taller players to get into the penalty area.		

Quote | 'The success I have at free kicks is 5% skill and 95% successful imagery.' (Gianfranco Zola)

'Imagery', 'visualization', 'mental rehearsal' and 'mental practice' are all common terms used to describe the process of using your imagination to see yourself performing, say, a free kick. If you are able to use all your senses to create an action in your mind before actually carrying out the activity, research has shown that there is more chance of success. This is also true for imagining a positive outcome to a match. If you think you will perform well, and see yourself performing well, you will generally perform well. Try using imagery yourself in different situations:

- **Before going to sleep at night.**
- **Pre-match.**
- **During training.**
- **During a break in matches.**
- **Just before you are about to take a corner, free kick or penalty.**

Summary

- **A good midfield player will have high energy levels and good all-round fitness, including stamina and speed.**

- **Midfield players will have the technical ability to defend, to keep possession through accurate passing, and also the flair and creativity to create and convert goal-scoring opportunities.**

- **Whether attacking or defending, midfield players are likely to have a key role in all set-play situations.**

- **Midfield players need to offer support all over the pitch. They need to support defenders when they are in possession and also get forward to support strikers as their team attacks.**

Self testers

1 When might a midfield player make a blind-side run?

2 Can you remember the top tip for switching play?

3 Name two good reasons why your team should use width in attacking situations.

Action plan

1 Discuss the tactics and ideas in this chapter with your coach and agree on a coaching plan for ten weeks.

2 Try to evaluate your performance so you can identify the areas of your game on which you may need to concentrate.

Part 4

Developing your game

Chapter 10

Parents, coaches and clubs

THIS CHAPTER WILL:
- Help you understand how important parents or carers are to your development as a player.
- Explain the roles played by the coach and parent.
- Show how you can work successfully with your coach.
- Give you guidance on choosing a club.

Parent power

One of the biggest influences on your football interest and involvement will be your parents or carers. Your coach or a teacher at school may fine-tune your dribbling skills and improve your passing techniques, but your parents will have the major impact on your desire, attitudes, values and ambitions.

Research has shown that the interest and support of parents is vital to a young player's participation in sport. It has, however, also shown that much of the pressure and anxiety that young players feel in sport comes from their parents. You need to be aware of this; some of the influence

of your parents on your football experience will be positive and constructive, but some will not.

Positive and negative effects

Most parents have the best intentions in mind when they support and help their child to become footballers, whether for the local park team or for a professional club. Nonetheless, these good intentions can lose their way as parents become involved with the emotional roller-coaster ride of junior football. We have all witnessed the parents who shout and scream from the touchline, following every movement of their own child, with no awareness of the other players in the team. Goals, results and their child's involvement in the game are all-important, with criticism as likely as encouragement when they talk to their child following a game. These types of parents believe that they are supporting their eight year old, but instead they are building up possible problems for that child. They probably mean well – they just want their son or daughter to succeed, but they become too animated and involved. So why does this happen?

Parents have a strong desire to 'make things right' for their son or daughter, but this can be taken too far, however well intentioned. A belief that there is a right and a wrong way to do things can lead to confrontation, for example, by telling a child what he or she should have done, rather than respecting them and encouraging them to work things out for themselves.

Many parents are re-living their sporting experience through their child, which is one reason why they want as many opportunities as possible open to their child. If their son or daughter fails, it is a reflection of their own sporting ability, or inability, and it is felt acutely. Once again, the intentions of trying to maximize opportunities are good but the effect when seen to be a failure can be negative. The pressure on a player of losing or playing badly can be doubled if their parent reacts in a frustrated and angry way.

■ It is not easy to be a good parent of a competitive football player. As a player you need to be aware of this, and encourage parents to:

- Be supportive without telling you how to do or not do something (unless you ask for help).

- Listen properly, without doing ten other things (parents are very busy people).

- Focus on the way you play and whether you're having fun and improving as a footballer.

- Motivate you to work hard and put in effort.

Quote | 'The importance of not pressuring athletes to "win early" in their careers, but to teach values such as hard work, optimism and a "can do" attitude seem paramount . . . At the same time, parents emphasised the attitude "if you are going to do it, do it right". They also modelled a hard work ethic, held high (but reasonable) expectations and standards for their child and emphasised a "stick to it" attitude.'

Dan Gould, *The Development of Psychological Talent in US Olympic Champions*, 2002

Role models

So, do parents still have an effect on you as a player as you get older? Certainly, the role a parent plays in the early years will help to shape your interest and attitude. This is not only through supporting you, but also through watching football in a wider sense. Sitting together to watch a match on television or going to a match together helps forge a bond and gives an opportunity to share thoughts on the way the game is played.

How do you think Gerrard played today?
Would you play Jones in that position?
Have you seen how much space their midfield has been allowed?
Do you think that was a fair tackle?

Informal chatting around questions like these helps you gain a keen understanding of the way the game is played, the positions, the attitudes, the pace, and the roles of the individual players within each team. This can all be related to your own experience as a player and will have an influence on the way you play.

All through your development as a player, you have hopefully had the backing and support of your parents. It may be in a small way, such as making your drink or washing your kit, or in a much greater way such as managing your team. As you mature and develop as a player, this role can be reversed, with you as a player giving your parents the opportunity to feel involved. After training, talk to them about the session. What did you learn? How did you feel? Was it an enjoyable session? Don't wait for questions; show them that you value their interest. After a match, talk about the way the game went, the highs and lows and, if they watched, ask them what they thought about the match. Try to be positive and you are likely to get a positive response.

Most importantly, you are the link between your coach and your parent. Any information given to you by your coach concerning dates of matches, kick-off times or changes to training needs to be passed on to your parents. It can be incredibly frustrating as a coach or manager if information isn't passed on and only six players turn up at a re-arranged match. This works both ways – any messages from your parents, perhaps concerning holidays away, need to be passed on to your coach or manager.

Coaching principles

Football coaches come in many shapes, sizes and styles, but they all share one quality: a desire to improve their players and their team. Some have more success than others in achieving this! All coaches have beliefs and opinions about what coaching is and how coaches can help players. Many will have been playing football for more years than they care to mention, others will be huge football fans with a fantastic knowledge about football. Some will be trained and qualified Football Association (FA) coaches, others will be willing volunteers with no qualifications but plenty of enthusiasm.

For all these types of coaches, much of their success or failure depends on their principles – their ethics, sense of fair play and their codes of behaviour. These have a direct impact on the players. You may have been a player in a number of teams, with a variety of different coaches, and each will have developed their own style of coaching. Think about your coach, or a coach from a previous team, and consider these questions about their coaching principles:

- Does the coach shout from the touchline? Is it constructive?
- Are you encouraged to enjoy the game?
- Is winning all-important?
- Are players punished for a poor performance?
- What is the view of your coach on swearing?
- Does the coach communicate well with all the players?
- What is the view of your coach on cheating?
- Are you encouraged to accept refereeing decisions?
- Do all players get a chance to play?

The principles of your coach will affect the way you play the game. The principles a coach upholds will be evident in their behaviour towards others and in how they expect you as a player to behave towards them. As well as shaping you as a footballer, you may want to coach a team in the future, so bear the following principles in mind.

Principles of successful coaching
- Respecting the needs of individuals and treating all players fairly.
- Developing independence by encouraging players and other coaches to accept responsibility for their own behaviour.
- The development of individuals as people as well as football players.
- The development of mutual trust, respect and commitment.
- Positive acknowledgement of progress and achievement.
- Communication with players, coaches, parents and other helpers.
- Promoting fair play within the Laws of the Game and respecting the dignity of opponents and officials.
- Accepting responsibility for the conduct of players and encouraging positive social and moral behaviours.
- Maintaining confidentiality of information when appropriate to do so.
- Displaying high personal standards of behaviour, dress and communication.
- Ensuring as far as possible the safety and health of players.
- Developing personal competence as a coach.

Based on the *FA Sport and Recreation Values Statement for Coaching, Teaching and Instructing*, 2000

Working with a coach

If you ask a coach what they value most in a player, many will state the ability to listen. Players are more likely to improve their skills and techniques by concentrating when they are asked to listen to any instructions. Any information or advice given is then internalized and can be transferred to the physical action. Obviously this can be a problem if the coach isn't particularly inspiring or if other players around have a poor attitude. However, this is an important life skill as it concerns a feeling of respect for others, and will say a lot about you as a person as well as a player. If you listen well, you are also likely to ask more questions, sharing the responsibility for improving yourself as a player and the team as a whole.

Talking to the coach, listening, asking questions – this is all about communication. It is a two-way process, and many players forget to respond positively to their coach. So be friendly and supportive, talk to the coach if things are going wrong or going well, and don't forget to thank your coach at the end of a training session or match.

Effort is another quality highly rated by coaches. If you work hard in training, try things out, and concentrate on improving your skills and technique, you will get more out of the training and are likely to increase your enjoyment. Show the same effort and commitment in matches and you will definitely be a valued team member for the other players and the coach. This is particularly true if things aren't going well in a match. If winning and losing is all-important, with too much emphasis placed on the result, it is very easy to 'give up' when being beaten. There is a sense of failure and some individuals are likely to withdraw their effort and behave in a negative way to 'protect' their own perceived ability at football. These 'ego-oriented' individuals see success in terms of winning and outperforming others, with even greater success if they put in little effort to win. A 'task-oriented' player sees success in terms of getting better by trying harder. Research has shown that the latter players will remain motivated even when they are losing because success is not based purely on the result, but on trying hard to improve. For example, a centre-forward who misses a few chances will continue to run into space in the attacking third of the field and accept the responsibility of taking shots at goal. If this is an 'ego-oriented' player, they are likely to put in less effort and drift further and further back after missing a few chances. Coaches find this behaviour difficult to understand, but it is often based on a player's early experiences playing in a team. It is not too late to change. It is also worth pointing out that top professional footballers have a mixture of high 'ego' and high 'task' orientation – they have a strong desire to win and put in a huge amount of effort to improve as a player. What sort of player are you – 'ego-oriented' or 'task-oriented'?

Choosing a club

Finding a football club that is right for you can be difficult and you are likely to need the support of your parents. The easiest option is to follow your friends to a particular club or to join your nearest one. Although this can often be the best reason for choosing a club, other factors should be considered. To begin with, think of the sort of football you want to play:

- **How much commitment do you want to give to training and matches?**
- **Are you able to play regularly on a Saturday or Sunday?**
- **How far are you willing to travel?**
- **What standard to you want to achieve?**
- **Do you want to play for a team that has a fun 'everyone plays' philosophy or do you want a competitive environment (or a bit of both)?**

Once you've considered this, make a list of the clubs that are available to you:

- **Contact your local County Football Association or local organization (theFA.com). They will be able to provide you with a list of clubs and programmes offered in your area.**
- **Ask friends and their parents for their views.**
- **Ask at your school as many clubs have developed excellent relationships with their local school.**
- **Look in the local press and/or the internet for contact details of clubs in your localilty.**

Once you are ready to contact or visit a club, find out the background information on the club by checking its website, looking at any brochures or by talking to club officials.

- Is the club affiliated to the local county football association? If so, this is a sign of good practice since unaffiliated football is not encouraged as it often lacks the appropriate insurance cover.
- How experienced and qualified are the coaches?
- Do they cater for a range of age groups for boys and girls?
- What are the facilities at the club like?
- Does the club have social and fund-raising events?
- What is the club's philosophy?
- What are the selection procedures? For example, does missing training mean that a player is left out of the team?
- Does the club have a Code of Conduct (see p. 256)?
- Does the club follow the FA child protection procedures? (This should be a definite yes!)
- Who are the club officials – chair, secretary, treasurer, etc?

In England the FA has a club recognition programme – Charter Standard Clubs. If a club you are looking at has this status, it will certainly help answer a lot of the questions above. To receive the FA Charter Standard kitemark, clubs must demonstrate safe, quality practice. This includes:

- Qualified coaches.
- Child protection trained staff and policy.
- Codes of conduct.
- Fair play.

The next step is to visit the club. Here are a few tips on what to look out for on your first visit perhaps to training or to watch a match:

- Is there a welcoming atmosphere?
- Do the players look like they are enjoying the football?
- Are there parents watching or do they keep away?
- What is the relationship like between the coach and players?
- Is there a good coach to player ratio? Generally, this should be two coaches per squad, with a maximum 1:16 ratio.

Top tip

Once you are a member of a team, try to become involved with the club in a broader way. Go along to any social events and support them in fund-raising. If they need volunteer help in, say, running a mini-soccer event, put your name forward. The more you become involved, the more you will get out of being part of the club.

Becoming a coach

You may have a desire to continue your interest in football beyond just playing the game. Coaching football is a tremendous way to give back to grassroots players some of the skills and attributes that you have developed over the years. Once you make a start on the coaching journey, you will become a valued member of the community, and it may even influence the path your career takes.

As soon as you reach 16 years of age, you can start your coaching development in England by taking the FA's level 1 coaching award. Although you may feel you have a good understanding of the game, the course looks at much more than just training drills and tactics and is a valuable exercise for anyone looking for a role in coaching. It is also the first rung on the ladder and an important one for providing you with the FA philosophy for coaches.

For those interested in coaching, Table 10.1 shows the development of courses and awards for coaches in England:

The FA Code of Conduct

The FA expects certain standards from all those involved in the game, whether players, officials, parents or coaches, at whatever level of play. A set of guidelines for clubs has been issued, which outlines the expected standards from the FA. This is set out below.

FA Code of Conduct for football

1 General

Football is the national game. All those involved with the game at every level and whether as a player, match official, coach or administrator, have a responsibility, above and beyond compliance with the law, to act according to the highest standards of integrity, and to ensure that the reputation of the game is, and remains high. This code applies to all those involved in football under the auspices of the Football Association.

2 Community

Football at all levels is a vital part of a community. Football will take into account community feelings when making decisions.

3 Equality

Football is opposed to discrimination of any form and will promote measures to prevent it, in whatever form, from being expressed.

4 Participants

Football recognizes the sense of ownership felt by those who participate at all levels of the game. This includes those who play, those who coach or help in any way, and those who officiate, as well as administrators and supporters. Football is committed to appropriate consultation.

Table 10.1 **FA Learning coaching course matrix**

Course	For whom	Prerequisites	Where
Coaching Level 1	Coaches of young players.	Open entry course for anybody aged over 16 years of age. You don't need any experience, just an interest in the game and motivation to improve your knowledge.	Locally run courses managed by County FAs as well as residentially run courses at approved FA centres.
Coaching Level 2	Coaches with some experience at any level with regular participation.	Open entry course for anybody aged over 16 years of age with regular practical experience of participation of football.	Locally run courses managed by County FAs as well as residentially run courses at approved FA centres.
Coaching Level 3 /UEFA 'B'	Coaches that are working with a team over an extensive period.	Anybody over 18 years of age. Candidates must hold the Level 2 Coaching Certificate.	Locally run courses managed by County FAs as well as residentially run courses at approved FA centres.
UEFA 'A'	Coaches with experience at representative level.	Candidates must hold the Level 3 /UEFA 'B' Certificate in Coaching.	Nationally run course that takes place residentially at approved FA centres.

For more information and to enrol on a course visit www.TheFA.com/FALearning

5 Young people

Football acknowledges the extent of its influence over young people and pledges to set a positive example.

6 Propriety

Football acknowledges that public confidence demands the highest standards of financial and administrative behaviour within the game, and will not tolerate corruption or improper practices.

7 Trust and respect

Football will uphold a relationship of trust and respect between all involved in the game, whether they are individuals, clubs or other organizations.

8 Violence

Football rejects the use of violence of any nature by anyone involved in the game.

9 Fairness

Football is committed to fairness in its dealings with all involved in the game.

10 Integrity and fair play

Football is committed to the principle of playing to win consistent with fair play.

FA Code of Conduct for coaches

1 Coaches are the key to the establishment of ethics in football. The concept of ethics and their attitude directly affects the behaviour of players under their supervision. Coaches are, therefore, expected to pay particular care to the moral aspects of their conduct. Coaches have to be aware that almost all of their everyday decisions and choices of actions, as well as strategic targets, have ethical implications.

2   It is natural that winning constitutes a basic concern for
    coaches. This code is not intended to conflict with that.
    However, the code calls for coaches to disassociate themselves
    with a 'win at all costs' attitude.

3   Increased responsibility is requested from coaches involved in
    coaching young people. The health, safety, welfare and moral
    education of young people are a first priority, before the
    achievement or the reputation of the club, coach or parent.

4   Set out below is the FA Coaches Association Code of Conduct
    (which reflects the standards expressed by the National Coaching
    Foundation and the National Association of Sports Coaches)
    which forms the benchmark for all involved in coaching:

    a   Coaches must respect the rights, dignity and worth of each
        and every person and treat each equally within the context
        of the sport.

    b   Coaches must place the well-being and safety of each
        player above all other considerations, including the
        development of performance.

    c   Coaches must adhere to all guidelines laid down by
        governing bodies.

    d   Coaches must develop an appropriate working relationship
        with each player based on mutual trust and respect.

    e   Coaches must not exert undue influence to obtain personal
        benefit or reward.

    f   Coaches must encourage and guide players to accept
        responsibility for their own behaviour and performance.

    g   Coaches must ensure that the activities they direct or
        advocate are appropriate for the age, maturity, experience
        and ability of players.

    h   Coaches should, at the outset, clarify with the players (and,
        where appropriate parents) exactly what is expected of
        them and also what they are entitled to expect from their
        coach.

i   Coaches must cooperate fully with other specialists (e.g. other coaches, officials, sports scientists, doctors, and physiotherapists) in the best interests of the players.

j   Coaches must always promote the positive aspects of the sport (e.g. fair play) and never condone violations of the laws of the game, behaviour contrary to the spirit of the laws of the game or relevant rules and regulations or the use of prohibited substances or techniques.

k   Coaches must consistently display high standards of behaviour and appearance.

l   Coaches must not use or tolerate inappropriate language.

FA Code of Conduct for players

1   Players are the most important people in the sport. Playing for the team, and for the team to win, is the most fundamental part of the game. But not winning at any cost – fair play and respect for others is of utmost importance.

2   This code is derived from one that focuses on players involved in top-class football. Nevertheless, the key concepts in the code are valid for players at all levels.

a   Obligations towards the game

A player should:

- Make every effort to develop their own sporting abilities, in terms of skill, technique, tactics and stamina.

- Give maximum effort and strive for the best possible performance during a game, even if his team is in a position where the desired result has already been achieved.

- Set a positive example to others, particularly young players and supporters.

- Avoid all forms of gamesmanship and time wasting.

- Always have regard for the best interests of the game, including where publicly expressing an opinion on the game and any particular aspect of it, including others involved in the game.

- Not use inappropriate language.

b Obligations towards one's own team

A player should:

- Make every effort consistent with fair play and the laws of the game to help his own team win.

- Resist any influence which might, or might be seen to, bring into question his commitment to the team winning.

c Respect for the laws of the game and competition rules

A player should:

- Know and abide by the laws, rules and spirit of the game, and the competition rules.

- Accept success and failure, victory and defeat, equally.

- Resist any temptation to take banned substances or use banned techniques.

d Respect towards opponents

A player should:

- Treat opponents with due respect at all times, irrespective of the result of the game.

- Safeguard the physical fitness of opponents, avoid violence and rough play. And help injured opponents.

e Respect towards match officials

A player should:

- Accept the decisions of the match officials without protest.

- Avoid words or actions that may mislead match officials.

- Show due respect towards match officials.

f Respect towards team officials

A player should:

- Abide by the instructions of their coach and team officials, provided they do not contradict the spirit of the code.

- Show due respect towards the team officials of the opposition.

g **Obligations towards the supporters**

A player should:

- Show due respect to the interests of supporters.

FA Code of Conduct for team officials

This code applies to all team/club officials (although some elements may not apply to all officials).

1 Obligations towards the game

The team official should:

- Set a positive example for others, particularly young players and supporters.

- Promote and develop his own team having regard to the interests of the players, supporters and reputation of the national game.

- Share knowledge and experience when invited to do so, taking into account the interest of the body that has requested this rather than personal interests.

- Avoid all forms of gamesmanship.

- Show due respect to match officials and others involved in the game.

- Always have regard for the best interests of the game, including where publicly expressing an opinion of the game and any particular aspect of it, including others involved in the game.

- Not use or tolerate inappropriate language.

2 Obligations towards the team

The team official should:

- Make every effort to develop the sporting, technical and tactical levels of the club/team, and to obtain the best results for the team, using all permitted means.

- Give priority to the interests of the team over individual interests.

- Resist all illegal or unsporting influences, including banned substances and techniques.

- Promote ethical principles.

- Show due respect for the interests of the players, coaches and officials, their own club/team and others.

3 Obligations towards supporters

The team official should:

- Show due respect for the interests of supporters.

4 Respect towards match officials

The team official should:

- Accept the decisions of the match officials without protest.

- Avoid words or actions that may mislead a match official.

- Show due respect towards match official.

FA Code of Conduct for parents/spectators

1 Parents/spectators have a great influence on children's enjoyment and success in football. All children play football because they first and foremost love the game – it's fun. Remember that however good a child becomes at football within the club it is important to reinforce the message to parents/spectators that positive encouragement will contribute to:

- Children enjoying football.

- A sense of personal achievement.

- Self-esteem.

- Improving the child's skills and techniques.

2 A parent's/spectator's expectations and attitudes have a significant bearing on a child's attitude towards:

- Other players.
- Officials.
- Managers.
- Spectators.

3 Parents/spectators will be positive and encouraging towards all children, not just their own.

4 Parents/spectators are encouraged to:

- Applaud the opposition as well as their own teams.
- Avoid coaching during the game.
- Refrain from shouting and screaming.
- Respect the referee's decisions.
- Give attention to each of the children involved in football, not just the most talented.
- Give encouragement to everyone to participate in football.

5 Parents and spectators should be made aware of these issues together with the club's other adopted codes of conduct and child protection policy.

Summary

- Your parents will have a major impact on your desire, attitudes, values and ambitions.

- Most parents start off with good intentions and may need your support to keep positive.

- Much of the success or failure of a coach depends on their principles – their ethics, sense of fair play and codes of behaviour.

- **Effort and good communication from players are highly valued by coaches.**

- **If you are in a position where you need to choose a club, put some time and research into choosing one that is right for you.**

Self testers

1 Think of three ways to involve your parents positively in your interest in football.

2 Describe some of the principles of successful coaching. Give four examples.

3 What are the requirements for a club to achieve Charter Standard in England?

Action plan

Consider your attitudes and behaviour during training sessions and matches. For the next four matches and training sessions, make a conscious effort to listen carefully, communicate more and put in more effort. Monitor the difference this makes to you as a player.

References

Motivation: More than a Question of Winning and Losing (1999), Darren C. Treasure, Assistant Professor of Sport and Exercise Psychology, Arizona State University

You may find the following books helpful:
The Official FA Guide: A Parent's Guide to Football by Les Howie
The Official FA Guide to Basic Team Coaching by Les Reed
The Official FA Guide to Basic Refereeing by John Baker
The Official FA Guide to Running a Club by Les Howie

Chapter **11**

Evaluating your performance

THIS CHAPTER WILL:
- Explain how a goal-setting programme can improve your game.
- Show the three stages for implementing a goal-setting programme.
- Give a practical example of a weekly goal-setting diary.

Goal-setting
Why set goals?

Sport psychologists have identified goal-setting as an effective way to help players prepare for competition and improve technical, physical and mental performance. It involves the establishment of specific targets that show what a player, with or without the involvement of a coach, is striving to achieve.

Goal-setting should be seen as a method of helping you develop areas of weakness and maintain your strengths. This chapter focuses specifically on the development of the individual rather than the team.

Table 11.1 **Types of goals**

Training goals

Training goals can improve performance by directing attention towards specific aspects of personal development as well as generating the effort needed to make progress.

Training goals are often organized through a framework that features long- and short-term goals (see below).

Long-term goals

These identify what a player or coach wants to achieve.

They are usually stated in general terms and reflect a player's aspirations and ambitions.

An example could be for a player to establish themselves as a 'regular' in his/her local team, or to successfully recover from an injury.

Competition goals

'Process' goals can be used to influence the way you approach games. They can focus on specific tasks before a match such as 'closing down quickly' or 'being aware of movement off the ball'.

It is important to focus your attention on the process rather than the outcome of the match.

Short-term goals

These are more precise and associated with daily/weekly 'action steps'.

Short-term goals and 'action steps' can influence what takes place at your team's training session or they may relate to your individual practice time.

Short-term goals relate to practical action which can lead towards reaching your long-term goals.

An example may be to improve short passing skills.

Types of goals

Statistic

Goal-setting and targets are used by professional football clubs to help the development of the players at their academies and centres of excellence.

It may be better understood if players think of the short-term and long-term goals as linked like a staircase (See Figure 11.1). At the top of the staircase is the long-term goal, with the short-term goals represented by the progression of stairs. Achieving short-term goals improves the likelihood that long-term goals will be reached.

Figure 11.1 **An example of a goal-setting staircase**

> **Establish myself as a 'regular' player in my local team**
>
> Maintain concentration for the full game
>
> Improve fitness level
>
> Improve accuracy of passing
>
> Improve communication on the pitch
>
> Improve ball control

In simple terms: commitment to action steps = short-term goals achieved = long-term goals realized.

Top tip

Be realistic! You need to be realistic about the amount of time and effort you can put into a goal-setting programme.

Three stages for implementing a goal-setting programme

Before setting a programme, it is important that you have spent some time evaluating your game – strengths, weaknesses and long-term goals. You can do this on your own or, even better, by involving a supportive parent or coach. The coach or parent can oversee the programme and alter and develop it over time.

Table 11.2 **Goal-setting stages**

Stage 1	Stage 2	Stage 3
Establish the way forward	*Set goals*	*Monitor, maintain and evaluate*
Meeting/discussion.	Goal-setting programme should come from the meeting/discussion.	Formal or informal meetings to reflect on progress and consider any changes.
Consider your strengths and weaknesses.		
The coach, if involved, should become familiar with your views about your own ability as well as any personal targets.	Establish long-term goals.	Whenever possible, record progress in writing.
Coach should share his/her views on how you could improve.	Identify short-term goals (what has to be done to reach the long-term goals).	Check the time you have given and how long it is taking to achieve short- and long-term goals.
	Make sure the goals are SMART: **S**pecific. **M**easurable. **A**chievable/Adjustable. **R**ealistic/Recorded. **T**ime phased.	This stage allows for new challenges and targets to be set.

Top tips

Make sure that when you set a goal programme, the goals are SMART.

Keeping a goal-setting diary

It is a good idea to keep a weekly goal-setting diary. Table 11.3 is an example of one that has been completed.

Table 11.3 **Weekly goal-setting diary**

Goal-setting diary   **Date:**
Short-term goal for this week:
Develop my short passing skills

Action steps   **Thoughts**
Monday

Work with team-mate/coach on   *Passing with my right foot is good,*
controlling and passing. Use both   *though I am still weak with my left.*
feet, two touch only.

Tuesday
No training

Wednesday

Five-a-side match with team-mates.   *My accuracy of passes has improved.*
Goal – I will try and play two touch *I enjoyed the match and was pleased*
when in possession.   *with my performance.*

Thursday

Team training session   *My passing was accurate and sharp,*
Coach to organize short passing drills. *particularly with my right foot. I am*
Goal: in drills I will play one touch. *starting to feel more confident.*

Friday

School match.   *Satisfied with my performance as short*
Goal – accurate passing and quick   *passing had improved though coach*
decisions on the ball.   *felt I could make quicker decisions.*

■　Use this model to start your own diary and develop action steps to implement your short-term goals.

Summary

- **Goal-setting can help you organize your training and ensure that important areas of development have a focus.**

- **It is important to establish long- and short-term goals for training and to use process-type goals as part of preparation for playing competitive football.**

- **Goal-setting should be written down and reviewed on a regular basis.**

- **The more effort that you put into your goal-setting programme, the greater the chance of success in improving your play.**

Self testers

1　What are the three key stages in a goal-setting programme?
2　Describe action steps.
3　What does SMART stand for?

Action plan

Consider planning your own goal-setting programme using the three-stage approach covered in this chapter. Start by planning a diary and arranging a meeting with your coach.

You may find *The Official FA Guide to Psychology for Football* by Dr Andy Cale useful.

Index

Master the Game
Striker

Achieve your potential

Master the Game: Striker gives you the skills and essential advice you need to perfect this key position. It helps you master the specific skills and techniques that are fundamental to becoming a great striker, and covers nutritional, fitness and psychological aspects of player performance.

This book enables you to:
- **understand the key principles of play**
- **prepare for the game**
- **improve your skills, from sharp shooting to agility**
- **learn from your match performance.**

Packed full of indispensable tips and techniques, this book will soon enhance your ability and increase your enjoyment of the world's greatest game.

Paul Broadbent is the manager and coach of an under-16s football team and a widely published author. **Andrew Allen** is a development manager for school sport and an FA qualified coach.

Master the Game
Defender

Achieve your potential

Master the Game: Defender gives you the skills and essential advice you need to perfect this key position. It helps you master the specific skills and techniques that are fundamental to becoming a great defender, and covers nutritional, fitness and psychological aspects of player performance.

This book enables you to:
- **understand the key principles of play**
- **prepare for the game**
- **improve your skills, from heading to tough tackling**
- **learn from your match performance.**

Packed full of indispensable tips and techniques, this book will soon enhance your ability and increase your enjoyment of the world's greatest game.

Paul Broadbent is the manager and coach of an under-16s football team and a widely published author. **Andrew Allen** is a development manager for school sport and an FA qualified coach.